PRAISE FOR Faith and th

Years ago, parents watched *Little House on the Prairie*. Today it's *Modern Family*. And the book you need to read if you're a parent in these crazy, modern times is Craig Jutila's book *Faith and the Modern Family*—from dealing with bad behavior, to guidance on carving out time for what's most important; from protecting your child online, to helping them find their purpose and knowing how to get there, help is here. This book is filled with humor, with "I've been there" stories that will grab your heart, and with biblical principles that will guide your modern family toward God's best--even in our "too modern," broken world.

John Trent, Ph.D.
President and Founder, StrongFamilies.com

I love Craig Jutila, and I love this book. Craig masterfully navigates the fine line between theory (every parent needs good guiding principles) and real-world help. While you'll find timeless principles in this book, it's also peppered with timely, practical, just-when-you-need-it advice. The section on knowing how to protect your child online is worth the purchase price alone. You'll keep this book handy for years to come.

Carey Nieuwhof
Lead Pastor of Connexus Church
Author, *Leading Change Without Losing It*; Coauthor, *Parenting Beyond Your Capacity*
www.careynieuwhof.com

Craig's book, *Faith and the Modern Family*, addresses the four areas that families are struggling with the most. In particular, the first section of the book will give every parent a plan to help his or her family live a balanced life together—something that is critically missing in today's world. If you are a parent who cares about the future of your family, you should definitely read *Faith and the Modern Family*.

Reggie Joiner
President and Founder, ReThink Group
www.whatisorange.com

Craig has a reputation for dealing with the issues that matter most to families . . . and here he has done it again. This book engages parents at the bedrock of their questions and fears. It offers sound, biblical advice and a no-nonsense approach to application. For anyone who is raising kids in a modern world (or thinking about it), this book is a must-have resource to have in arm's reach at all times.

Michelle Anthony
Family Ministry Architect, David C. Cook
Author and Communicator, www.michelleanthony.org

Once again Craig has hit the ball out of the park with a must-read for every parent. Here's a book that gives practical answers to how to cultivate true faith in today's modern family. I appreciate Craig's honesty and also his willingness to make a difference where it matters the most—at home. This is not only a book to read, but also a book to share with others. If families will apply the principles and insights Craig and Mary give us from their own story, they will find all that God desires for their families.

Jim Wideman
Teacher, Author and Ministry Consultant
www.jimwideman.com

I love the insight and practical help for parents who are trying to figure out how to raise kids in today's busy digital and social world. With wisdom and humor, Craig offers practical steps to help parents navigate this world. Every parent needs a copy of this book.

Sue Miller
Coauthor, *Making Your Children's Ministry the Best Hour of Every Kid's Week;*
Creative Team Member, ReThink Group

One of the things I love about Craig and the way he writes is his straight-forward, down-to-earth, practical approach. This book is filled with simple and doable ideas that will truly help you establish and raise a healthy family in the modern world in which we live.

Mark Holmen
Author, *Faith Begins at Home*
National and International Consultant and Speaker, Faith at Home Movement
www.faithathome.com

Craig continues to be a leading voice on creating healthy parameters for the over-extended family. This book is a must-read for parents navigating the waters of today's modern world.

Michael Chanley
Creator CMConnect.org
Executive Director, International Network of Children's Ministry
www.INCM.org

faith
and the
modern
fami*ly*

How to Raise a **Healthy Family**
in a "Modern Family" World

craig jutila

Regal

For more information and
special offers from Regal Books, email us at
subscribe@regalbooks.com

Published by Regal
From Gospel Light
Ventura, California, U.S.A.
www.regalbooks.com
Printed in the U.S.A.

Library of Congress Cataloging-in-Publication Data

Jutila, Craig, 1965-
Faith and the modern family : how to raise a healthy family in a modern family world /
Craig Jutila.
pages cm
Includes bibliographical references.
ISBN 978-0-8307-6866-0 (trade paper)
1. Families—Religious life. 2. Parenting—Religious aspects—Christianity. 3. Child rearing—Religious aspects—Christianity. 4. Families—Religious aspects—Christianity. I. Title.
BV4526.3.J88 2014
248.4—dc23
2013040129

Rights for publishing this book outside the U.S.A. or in non-English languages are administered by Gospel Light Worldwide, an international not-for-profit ministry. For additional information, please visit www.glww.org, email info@glww.org, or write to Gospel Light Worldwide, 1957 Eastman Avenue, Ventura, CA 93003, U.S.A. To order copies of this book and other Regal products in bulk quantities, please contact us at 1-800-446-7735.

Dedication

This book is dedicated to my family, the most important people in my life: those who breathe life into me, challenge me and understand me the best. They see my weaknesses and love me anyway; they see my mistakes and love me anyway; they see my faults and love me anyway. As a husband and a dad, I am grateful for my family not because of what they do but because of who they are.

To my wife Mary: my high school sweetheart, the love of my life and my soul mate. We have laughed until we have cried and we have cried until we have laughed. Through the ups and downs on the roller coaster of life, there is no one I would rather have next to me than you! You encourage me and you balance me and I love you deeply.

To Alec: You make me laugh and you make me laugh out loud! Sometimes when I am in the car by myself, I will remember something you said and start laughing or smiling. I wish I had your self-esteem when I was in high school. You are both logical and practical and you are making a difference in this world. I can't wait to see how your influence expands as you continue your journey. I love you.

To Cameron: You help me express empathy and compassion. So many times I have seen you show kindness and reach out to make others feel like they belong. You have taught me to feel deeply and think wisely. God is on the move in your life and I have a front row seat to see what amazing things He is going to do through you. "I am confident of this very thing, that He who began a good work in you will perfect it until the day of Christ Jesus" (Phil. 1:6, *NASB*). I love you.

To Karimy: You help me stand up for what I believe. Your efforts to share Jesus with your friends or invite people to church or serve the poor all come out of your heart. Your desire for others to know Jesus makes me stronger as your dad. Your persistence helps you move forward regardless of the obstacles in your way, and your desire to help others gives you the grace to impact this world in a powerful way. I love you.

Contents

Preface

The ideas in this book are already impacting families. Use the following link to hear some of their stories:

http://www.whowillyouempower.com/fmofy.

Introduction

Parenting Your Modern Family

Times are changing, especially for families. Today's modern family is facing challenges that rarely, if ever, crossed our minds a few years ago, and in some cases, a few months ago!

Most families today are long on commitment and short on time and are being pulled in so many directions that it makes it difficult, if not impossible, to connect face-to-face. Smartphones, mobile technology, work-life balance, relentless hurry and stress seem to be woven into the fabric of our lives. If these things are true, the question that begs to be answered is, How do parents raise a healthy family in a modern world?

In the hit ABC TV comedy series *Modern Family*, the dad, Phil Dunphy, is being interviewed as part of the episode. The question posed to him is, "What's the key to being a great dad?"

Phil: "Be their buddy."
Claire (*Phil's wife, popping out from behind the wall*): "Seriously, is that your answer?"
Phil (*Nervously starts to rattle off a few more options*): "Stay in school. Don't do drugs. Just give me the answer!"[1]

I certainly remember my first mission trip with a group of kids from church. We made the drive from Southern California to Del Rio, Texas, and then into Acuna, Mexico. I can remember being rushed around to different churches and being warmly greeted, but not knowing a lick of Spanish—I mean, *nada*. We had arrived late to the first church we visited and it was already packed. The only pew left was the one in the front row. So, as the pastor, I was taken to the front row.

Church was radically different from what I was used to, so I picked someone out of the crowd to kind of watch and imitate. The man sitting next to me on the front pew seemed to know what he was doing, so I followed him. As everyone sang, the man clapped his hands, so I clapped my hands. When the man stood up to pray, I stood up to pray. When the man sat down, I sat down. When the man held the cup and bread for the Lord's Supper, I held the cup and bread. During the preaching, I did not understand a thing. I just sat there and tried to look just like that man in the front row.

After the service was over, I thought the preacher was making some announcements. The people clapped, so I looked over to see if that guy was clapping, and he was; so I clapped too. Then the preacher said some more words that I didn't understand, and then I saw the man next to me stand up. So I went ahead and stood up too. All of a sudden a hush fell over the entire congregation. A few people let out audible gasps. I looked around and saw that nobody else was standing. Then I looked at the guy I had been imitating, and he was staring at me with an angry expression. So I sat down.

After the service ended, the pastor stood at the door to shake the hands of those who were leaving. When I went to the back to greet the pastor, he said to me in English, "I guess you don't speak Spanish." I told him that I didn't and asked him if it was so obvious: The pastor said, "Yep, because at the end of the service I announced that the Acosta family had a newborn baby boy and would the proud father please stand up."

Have you ever felt that way about parenting? You look at someone who you think is a good dad or a good mom and you start modeling how that person parents. You stand when he or she stands; you clap when he or she claps; you read what he or she reads. Or maybe, like Phil Dunphy, you just want someone to give you the answer.

I can remember the night when I brought my wife home after giving birth to our twin boys. One of our sons, Alec, needed to stay in the neonatal intensive care unit (NICU), but we brought home our other son, Cameron, that night. It was 1:00 in the morning. We were tired. But there was a quiet calmness in that moment as we sat staring at each other. Mary was holding Cameron and rocking him. Suddenly, I felt the quiet move from a whisper to a conversation to a full panic attack inside me. I blurted to Mary, "Hon, we have no idea what we are doing, do we?"

When she just smiled quietly at me and then looked back down into Cameron's face, the calmness returned. We have been on the parenting journey ever since.

The difficulty for me in writing a book on raising a healthy family is simply this: There are times when I am not a good parent. In fact, I should probably tell my kids, "Hey, did you guys just see what Dad did? Okay, don't do that."

I really want this book to be more about what kids need from us as parents rather than what a good parenting philosophy is. To me, parenting isn't a one-size-fits-all concept. Each of us is wired differently, and each of our children is wired differently. I really like what Psalm 78:72 says: "He cared for them with a true heart and led them with skillful hands." Although this is not a verse about parenting, I like what it says, and I think we can apply it to how we parent. What if we cared for our kids, our families, with a true heart and in a skillful manner?

Mary and I have always told our kids that we love them and want the absolute best for them. We have also told them that, as parents, we may be wrong on occasion. We all make mistakes, even parents. It seems a bit unfair in life that we get ample time to practice just about everything we do except parenting.

In becoming parents, a married couple enters into one of the most important, if not *the* most important, seasons of life; yet, there is no practice test, no long-term schooling or mentoring program, no manual, no application process or on-the-job training.

Think about it: We practice after school for our sports teams in order to develop chemistry and skill. We take practice tests on a Tuesday so that we can get a feel for what will be asked on the actual test on Friday. We take practice SAT tests so that when it comes time for the real thing we are better prepared. We practice for months to learn the rules of the road and how to navigate traffic on the streets before taking our driver's test. Yet, when it comes to parenting, training seems to be optional.

There is a definite skill set to parenting, especially in this "modern family" world. I used to have a slightly different mindset about this, but technology and the ever-increasing speed of life require parents who are not only aware but also skilled in the difficulties and opportunities presented to the family in today's modern world. If not, then they may end up asking their eight-year-old how he accessed that inappropriate content on the Web, and could he please block himself (or herself) from any further inappropriate activity or content.

There are, of course, many topics that could be discussed when it comes to today's modern family. However, there are four recurring questions—four themes:

1. How do we find time together as a family?
2. How can we help our kids with their behavior?
3. How do we understand the power of the Internet in our kids' lives?
4. How can we move our family into a healthy future?

If you are a parent of teenagers, you may be saying, "Yes, we are dealing with those topics on a daily basis!"

If you are a parent of a young child, you may be saying, "Do we really have to deal with those topics right now?"

If you are getting ready to become a parent, you may be saying, "Maybe we should wait, because we don't want to deal with those topics at all!"

Whether you are now a parent or soon will be, parenting isn't easy. When Mary and I left the hospital with our twin boys, we weren't given a manual, a mentor or a motivational speech. "Goodbye," was the parting word. We simply went home with these brand-new lives we were now responsible for. We weren't prepared; in fact, we were downright scared.

Mary and I have since added a girl to our family, and although our three children have been raised in the same environment with the same value system and the same rules all of their lives, they are different. To that I say, "Thank God!" Each of them has a unique outlook and perspective on life. One child may push a little harder, while another may be more compliant; one may be an introvert, while another doesn't care very much about what others think. Each child is unique in personality, skill, demeanor and experience. I say all that to make a point.

When Mary and I speak at a conference, we often get asked questions that start with, "What do you do when . . ." I want to tell you up front that I cannot answer that question. In fact, both Mary and I have asked that same question. Fortunately, we have been extremely blessed with friends who do life with us. We get together, share problems, hurts and concerns; and, in many cases, we ask each other, "What did you do when . . .?" And then we listen for feedback—what worked and what didn't work. We receive encouragement, support and a few nuggets we take back and try to implement in our family. (To be perfectly honest, I tend to avoid people and books that tell me their way is *the* way to do something. I prefer people and books that tell me there is *a* way to do something. I hope this book comes across as *a* way, not *the* way on the topic of parenting and family.)

You may say, "Craig, it sounds like you don't really know what you are doing." Yes! You got it. Well, sort of. Truth be told, I have 47 years of experience when it comes to parenting. That's the combined number of my children's ages and also includes hours and hours of study, research, teaching and training on the topic. As I said, we have three kids, but we didn't get practice kids. We mess up, blow it, seek advice, read books, go to conferences and pray daily for our children.

In this book, I want to share our experiences while on our parenting journey—what has worked, what would or could work, and what simply hasn't worked. There are some things we can all work on and apply as parents to help our children with their behavior so that they can grow into mature, healthy, independent adults. I want to do my best to answer the four questions that most families seem to be asking these days and, not so coincidentally, focus on what the Bible has to say and how it plays an integral part in today's modern family.

Our families will continue to evolve, morph and adapt as our calendars fill up, life overflows and technology gets "smarter." But the one component that stabilizes and balances all the change is faith. Faith, as Hebrews 11:1 explains it, "is the confidence that what we hope for will actually happen; it gives us assurance about things we cannot see." God has a plan for you, as a parent, and for your children. "They are plans for good and not for disaster, to give you a future and a hope" (Jer. 29:11).

There will be times as a parent when you just don't know what to do or what to say. It's in those difficult moments when you put faith into the mix of your modern family.

PART 1

What Should I Feed My Time-Starved Kids?

Set a Healthy Life Pace

Before I married, I had three theories about raising children and no children. Now, I have three children and no theories.
JOHN WILMOT, ENGLISH NOBLEMAN AND POET

Is raising a family today easier or harder than ever before? I have received lots of different responses to that question and, surprisingly, the answers are split about 50-50. Although we may find it difficult to agree on whether parenting is easier or harder these days, I think we would all agree that it's different.

Let me give you some context. Do you remember records? Yes, those round vinyl disk things that my children called big CDs when they first saw them several years ago. I can remember Alec telling me, "Dad, those will never fit in the computer."

How about eight-tracks? Not the number of lanes that are on that dirt thing at the local high school. No, I'm talking about those small and boxy little inventions that allowed us to listen to music in our cars from something other than the radio.

Fast forward (no pun intended) to the cassette days. This was the first time we could really put together a "best of" compilation of all our music from the 80s—I mean, from the past. If you had patience, and one of those big CDs (i.e., a vinyl record) and a cassette recorder, you were in business.

Don't forget the CD. It's already in the past as well. Who buys CDs anymore? My son Cameron returned home from a community garage sale with 10 CDs he bought for $1.00. And they were good CDs! I won't elaborate on the bands he brought home, but he went on a long Journey to get them. When he arrived at the sale, he felt like a Foreigner from another neighborhood. After all, he had to walk through some pretty tall Styx to get there. He caught an REO Speedwagon to make it back home on time. (Do you remember any of those groups?)

We have now moved beyond the CD into the age of digital media, and it's literally changing the way we think. I'm not talking about thinking differently. I'm talking about a subtle rewiring of our brains.

Most of us were taught to read books from left to right, largely in part because we held books in our hands, and our English language is written from left to right. This is not necessarily the way kids who have grown up using the Web read.

According to Nicholas Carr, American writer on technology and culture, children who have grown up using the Internet (Generation Net) take in and process information differently: "They don't necessarily read a page from left to right and from top to bottom. They might instead skip around, scanning for pertinent information of interest."[1]

When I was a child, I had to look for things to do. Today's modern family doesn't have to look for anything to do; things come looking for them! Push notifications on your smartphone, tablet or computer not only collect information for you but also tell you when it finds it! When I was growing up, a push notification was called a doorbell. This alerted me to the fact that a friend was at the door and probably wanted to play outside. Today's modern family has lost three things: the doorbell, playing and outside. Today's doorbell is an alert message on a gaming console, and playing with others is online rather than outside.

I just finished watching a promotion for the new Xbox One, which should be out by the release of this book. The advertisement begins with a question: "How does it [the Xbox One] give me the content I want faster?" The rest of the advertisement goes on to tell me how. It appears that life doesn't seem to be slowing down any time soon; if anything, the modern family seems to be caught in a gravity pull toward the desire to do more at a faster pace. If this is true, then a great question for each modern family to ask itself is, "What is a healthy life pace for us?"

We can no longer sit back with a foot dangling in the water and traverse the streams of daily activity as we leisurely go with the flow. Today, if we want to go with the flow, we will find ourselves capsized and gasping for air underneath the rapids of relentless hurry. Life has lost its healthy flow, like a river that has risen above its natural boundaries. We are flooded with information, and our lives have become overly saturated with busyness. The pace of life has quickened to such an extent that it has become important for every family to set a pace that is healthy.

A few years ago, I started thinking differently about this seemingly relentless push we all face. As a result, my family implemented five things that have helped us with our life pace; I believe these principles can help your family, too: (1) define your season; (2) work at work; (3) live end to end; (4) know your boundaries; and (5) simply simplify.

Define Your Season

Mary and I have talked extensively about the principle of seasonality in our book *Hectic to Healthy,* and it's worth mentioning here. The pace of your life should be determined by the season you are in, not the opportunities available to you in the moment. All of us have different seasons in our families. Some couples are married with no children and are thinking about starting a family. Some are married with one child, and others are married with two or more children. Some families are single-parent families or blended families.

Seasons come and seasons go. Each family is different from other families, and each season of their family life is different. Each season requires something different from them as parents and as a family.

Our season in the Jutila household is married with three kids—three teenagers, to be exact. Some would call that a cold winter season, while others would describe it as beautiful spring. We value humor and laughter in our home, so I would like to exercise that value here with a quote about teenagers from one of my favorite comedians, Jeff Allen: "I think one day God looked down over His creation and said, 'Hey, let's see how they like it to create someone in their own image that denies their existence.' I have looked everywhere in the Bible, and nowhere does it say how old the devil was when he rejected God's authority, but my guess is 15."

Okay, back to seasons. In the Bible, this concept of seasonality is best seen when Jacob says to his brother, Esau, "Please, my lord, go ahead of your servant. We will follow slowly, at a pace that is comfortable for the livestock and the children. I will meet you at Seir" (Gen. 33:14).

The "we" in this verse refers to Jacob's family. When Esau asked Jacob to come back home with him, Jacob politely declined the offer. Why? Because Jacob had defined his season. Jacob's season was in a family-with-small-children season, and he paced his family life accordingly. Notice the reason Jacob declined Esau's offer: It was for his family. Jacob knew it would be unhealthy for his family to travel at a breakneck speed. Jacob's response is something we should all take to heart when considering the speed at which our families travel through life. The goal of considering seasonality is to make decisions for our family within the context of it.

Jacob's season of life was married with kids. His family's season defined his time commitments, priorities, decisions and speed. Jacob knew that traveling at a speed that might be healthy for him but not for his children would put his family at risk, and I'm pretty sure he didn't have a smart phone. Would the answer have been different if Jacob had been single? Maybe, but we'll never know. What we do know is that his decision matched his life's season, and it was a healthy choice.

Seasons come and go. Our children come and eventually go. They go off to college or into a career, but they do go. We have limited time with them in our home. It's hard for me to quantify or "feel" time, so I need a little help. You could call it a reminder from time to time on how much time I have left with my kids in the home.

There is a scene that takes place in the kitchen of ABC's TV comedy *Modern Family* and that opens with chaos brewing. It's parents at their worst and the kids not much better. There is shouting, a fire erupting on the stove and a dish shattering as it hits the floor. Frenetic energy fills the scene as the dialogue picks up . . .

> Haley: "You win the award for the worst mother ever."
> Claire: "I will be sure to thank you in my speech."
> Haley: "I hope the whole house burns down."
> Mitchell (*Claire's brother, just arriving*): "Did we come at a bad time?"
> Claire: "Come back in seven years and five months when they are all gone."[2]

It's Claire's line that makes this scene actually pretty funny. She knew exactly how much time was left in her "I have kids in my house" season. I'm not sure how she had that information at the tip of her tongue, but it's actually pretty useful information

I would like to suggest a more practical and compelling way to track how much time you have left with your children in the home. It's called the Legacy Countdown, and it's an app created by the great folks at The ReThink Group. (Search the Apple App store for Legacy Countdown.)[3]

With this app on your smart phone (and/or your iPad), you can enter your child's name, age and expected graduation date, and the app will show you how much time you have left with your child before he or she goes off to college or to work. When you visualize the time you have left with your kids, there is a better chance of your making that time really count.

The frustration we sometimes feel when our own home scene erupts into chaos is fleeting when we look at those difficult times within the context of a season that's about to end. When you reach the time when your children have grown up and have moved out or away, you will wish for the walls to be dirty or to see crumbs on the floor or a messy room with laundry piled high. You will yearn for that broken glass and spilled milk or the fingerprints on the glass door or window. Time moves fast, and seasons transition quickly. Define your season, and live accordingly.

Work at Work

I remember coming home from work one evening several years ago and walking directly from the garage to the kitchen counter without saying hi to anyone. I put down my backpack, took out my laptop, opened my email and started to write. After a few minutes, my then five-year-old son Alec asked me what I was doing. I told him I didn't get all my work done at the office, so I needed to finish a few things at home. After a short pause, he said, "Well, maybe they can put you in a slower group at work." Well said!

How many of us secretly want to be put into a slower group at work? In the coming pages, I will talk about living life "end to end" vs. "and to and," but first I want to talk about leaving work at work. I know that is hard to do. One of the biggest mistakes I made in the last 15 years was working around the clock.

A work schedule that is specifically defined may be a bit easier than if your job feels like it doesn't have a start and end time. For example, if you work in retail, most likely you have a start time and end time, and once you leave your place of employment for the day, you are finished. It may be easier to leave work at work.

If your job is more loosely defined when it comes to starting and stopping time, it can be harder to leave work at work. For example, if you are a counselor, and you get a call after "quitting time," do you tell the person in crisis, "I'm sorry, I can't talk to you now; I have already finished work for today"? The line is not as black and white.

What if an idea pops into your mind that will help your position at work or advance a cause you are working to improve? Do you pull out your smartphone or tablet and jot down that idea? Do you pull out a napkin and pen (old school, right!) and write down that million-dollar idea? Again, the line gets a little blurry, doesn't it?

Of course, there are exceptions to any rule, and the opportunities of our modern technology further blur the lines because we are rarely, if ever, totally unplugged. You don't really ever completely leave work because when you do, work comes looking for you: emails to your smartphone; a text from your boss or an employee; a direct message from Twitter; or a Facebook alert. Work is always on, if you want it to be.

Perhaps we all need to add a switch to our smartphones that would put us in a "fun" mode or "stop" mode—a button similar to "airplane mode" that would simply disconnect us from contact for a time. Or maybe we could reverse our thinking to get a larger view of our family and our world. Here is a great story that illustrates this point:

> Each night when she came home from work, Gina spent an hour playing with her six-year-old daughter, Amanda. Everything else came second: dinner, chores and even Amanda's homework. Playtime was a ritual. But one night, Gina had to bring home extra work; playtime with Amanda would have to wait. Looking around for something to occupy her daughter, Gina found a magazine with a world map on its cover. She tore the map into pieces and spread them on a table. "Once you've put the puzzle together, we can play," she said, assuming the task would keep Amanda busy for hours.
>
> A half-hour later, Amanda announced she was finished, and sure enough, she had pieced together the entire map. "How did you do that?" her mom asked. "It was easy, Mommy," Amanda replied. "There was a picture of a family on the back, and when I put the family together, the whole world just fell into place."[4]

Amanda may be on to something. When we put the family together, the world just seems to come together.

Live End to End

Modern culture allows us to live in a way that keeps us not only physically busy but mentally and emotionally busy as well. I can remember growing up playing three different sports because each sport had its own season. There was a beginning to the season and an end. Today there is often a beginning, but rarely is there an end to any sport or activity.

When we were children, life offered us fewer choices. I had one video game: Pong. That was the extent of my video game choice. I couldn't play my video game with friends from another country or even from around the corner. To me, the world was big and slow. You and I were, in some ways, forced to live life end to end. Take a look at what could have been a typical parent schedule 30 years ago.

Drive Kids to School **THEN** Arrive at Office **THEN** Make a Call **THEN** Answer Mail

7:30am..9:00am

Life happened end to end, because it was the only way it could be done. You couldn't start a work-related phone call at home and walk out to your car to continue the conversation—unless, of course, you went to Radio Shack and bought one of those 50-foot phone cords, but that would only get you to the car, not down the street! Once you got to the office, you could make a call or answer mail. No, not email, just mail. You remember mail, don't you? Those paper envelopes delivered to a little box outside your house or to your office?

Living life end to end had its advantages. There were natural boundaries built into life, which meant we didn't need to think about them too much. Today's modern family has a vast array of choices. We are compelled to set healthy boundaries or suffer the consequences of busyness, hurry and out-of-pace living.

When our culture made a drastic change in the way families spend their time, when we gained the capability of living life on multiple layers at the same time, we didn't live life *end to end* anymore. We can and, in many ways, *must* live life *and to and*.

There are benefits to both ways of living. However, there is more potential for an unhealthy pace of life with the latter.

Take a look at a typical parent schedule from 7:30 A.M. to 9:00 A.M. It could look something like this:

Drive Kids to School............................**AND**
Start Working.......................................**AND**
Make a Call..**AND**
Answer E-Mail.....................................**AND**

7:30am...8:00am..9:00am

See how much we can do in such a short amount of time when we live life "and to and"? Our ability has outpaced our capacity, and that leads to a question for each of us to consider: Has our capacity for doing more increased?

As I process that question, I am inclined to say no, it hasn't. Our capacity hasn't changed, but our ability to reach it has. If you have a 16-ounce glass and want to pour 18 ounces into it, you most certainly can. However, as we all know, a 16-ounce glass holds 16 ounces, and no more. So, if you choose to pour 18 ounces into a 16-ounce glass, you will have a 2-ounce mess.

Let's change the glass example to a time example. We all have 24 hours in a day. What if we want to pour 26 hours worth of things to do into our 24-hour day? Here is the answer you have been waiting for. Are you ready? I don't know.

I honestly don't know. There are too many moving parts to consider. I wish I knew the answer. In fact, I think the answer is different for every family. Think back to what we just talked about: the concept of seasonality. Your capacity as a family should correspond to what season you are in. The answer to how much is too much seems to be a bit of a moving target.

With that in mind, I want to ask, and attempt to answer, three questions that will help us understand the value of living at capacity, not over it:

1. Are You Vulnerable?

"A person without self-control is like a city with broken down walls" (Prov. 25:28). A person or a family that can't control their ability to do or to filter out what would cause them to go over capacity is in a vulnerable position. Although it's not common for cities to build physical walls for protection these days, the Proverbs verse is a reminder to have at least some protection from intrusion. If you don't exercise some self-control with your ability to do more, you will put yourself and your family in a vulnerable position. Setting healthy boundaries, which I will talk about in the next point, is a healthy place to start.

2. Are You Capable?

"Practice self-control, and keep your minds clear so that you can pray" (1 Pet. 4:7, *GOD's WORD*). There has never been a time in our lives when we have been more capable of doing many things. Our ability has outpaced our capacity with information and options so readily available that compete for our time.

I wonder if Peter really knew the implications of what he was writing in the verse just referenced. I certainly believe God did, as He inspired Peter to write these compelling words; but do you think Peter understood the relevancy of them for us today? Did he look 2,000 years ahead and say, "I really hope these words will help Martin and Debbie as they raise their children in a modern world with a steady barrage of text messaging and push notifications"? Honestly, I don't think it crossed his mind. But—and here is the really amazing thing—God did see it. He knew where you and I would be, and these words fit perfectly for our modern families. The Bible's words are timeless!

Let me paraphrase what Peter said: "Just because you hear that alert for an incoming text doesn't mean you have to answer it. If you do, it will cause your mind to think differently. It will cause your mind to think in short bursts and to be in a constant state of on-off, on-off thinking, and that's okay on occasion, but not as a way of life. Take some time to keep your mind free of clutter; keep it clear. I want you to do this so that you can focus on the One to whom you are praying, so that you can reduce the noise and clutter that can force you to live over capacity."

3. Are You Suceptible?

"Someone may say, I'm allowed to do anything, but not everything is helpful. I'm allowed to do anything, but I won't allow anything to gain control over my life" (1 Cor. 6:12, *GOD'S WORD*).

Just because we can do something (ability) doesn't mean we should (capacity). Just because we can live life and-to-and doesn't mean we should. When we were growing up, we weren't as susceptible to doing more, simply because we had fewer choices. Our modern families are more susceptible to going over capacity because our ability to do so has increased. Today's modern family must filter out what is right for them and leave the rest. We are not talking about making choices to do either bad or good. If it were that simple, we would all be doing fine.

Today, our susceptibility is about making a choice between good and better. How do you say no to something that is good, helpful, life giving and healthy? Well, first you need to know where your family is going and what your family is committed to be. I will talk about this in detail in the last section of this book. However, if you are prone to a short attention span, feel free to flip over to chapter 10 and read about taking some practical steps to write your family's purpose statement. When you know what your family is all about, it's easier to say no to good and yes to better.

I will admit that I love technology! I love what it can do for the family, for God's kingdom, for church services and for business meetings. New technology will continue to open amazing possibilities for all of us, but we must be careful how we use it. Voltaire said, "With great power comes great responsibility."[5] And before Voltaire uttered his words, Jesus said, "When someone has been given much, much will be required in return; and when someone has been entrusted with much, even more will be required" (Luke 12:48). We are living in a modern world where much has been given and much is required, including our choice between what is good and what is best for our family.

No Your Boundaries

That subhead is not a typo. "No'ing" where your boundaries are as a family most often consists of setting limits. Setting limits in today's modern world of too many choices usually involves saying that little word "no." A family boundary is something you set that indicates a healthy limit for your family.

Here are a few questions that represent the myriad of activities common to most families. Discuss these questions with your family and work on coming up with some healthy family boundaries:

- How many sports can [name(s) of your child (children)] be involved in at one time?
- How many times should our family have dinner together each week?
- How much homework is appropriate each school day?

- How many outside activities can [insert name(s)] be involved in at one time?
- What time should I, as a parent, be home from work?
- How much TV time is allowed each day?
- How much computer or phone time is appropriate each day?

Feeding children a healthy life pace most definitely requires setting a few boundaries. A healthy diet is not only built on what you eat, but also on what you don't eat! Taking steps now to define a few boundaries is much easier than trying to make some up on the fly.

I know for a fact our kids love boundaries. Okay, I know what you may be thinking after that statement: *Yeah, right! Kids don't like boundaries. They are always pushing against them!* I know. That's why I said our kids like them! Our three children seem to get great satisfaction from pushing those boundaries to their full potential. I can only assume from the energy, excitement and enthusiasm they demonstrate when standing in front of a family boundary, that naturally they love them. They seem to get such great satisfaction out of pushing against each and every one that Mary and I set up.

Think of it this way: All children push the boundaries. If they had a job at their age, they would be paid to push the boundaries. They would get up, take a shower, change and go to work—pushing-boundaries work.

Several years ago, a theorist decided to try an experiment:

He decided to take down the chain-link fence that surrounded the nursery school yard. He thought the children would feel more freedom of movement without that visible barrier surrounding them. When the fence was removed, the children huddled near the center of the play yard. Not only did they *not* wander away; they didn't even venture to the edge of the grounds. Clearly, there is a security for all of us in defined boundaries.[6]

Boundaries are essential for families who desire to have a healthy life pace because boundaries define your space. Notice I said "your space." Think of having boundaries as your space for your pace.

Here are three examples of effective boundaries:

1. Our children will play one sport at a time.
2. Our entire family will have dinner together three times a week.
3. We will not say yes or commit to anything until we have discussed it together.

Take a few moments and brainstorm a few boundaries that could help create some space for your family's pace; then discuss them together. As you talk about the healthy boundaries that are right for your family, consider these three things:

1. *Your family boundaries are individual!*
   They are *for your family alone.* They are different from every other family's boundaries. For instance, a healthy no for your family could be another family's healthy yes.
2. *Your family boundaries are identifiable!*
   They should be *written down and visible*, because you won't be able to stay within your boundaries if you can't remember them.
3. *Your family boundaries are intentional!*
   Make sure you *deliberately address a need in your family.* The more specific you are with your wording, the more effective the boundary will be.

Once you establish a few healthy boundaries, you will notice things begin to change. Please understand, things won't change overnight; they will change over time. You will most likely experience a bit of negative feedback from your children, whose lives are suddenly altered. However, after the initial shock has worn off, you will all experience a less rushed and more focused family life.

If you have teenagers in the home, why not involve them in the conversation? Ask for their input and they will be more likely to get on board with family boundaries and do so with a good attitude.

The boundaries you set will protect your family from relentless hurry and protect your family's physical, mental, social and emotional space from intrusion. They also will protect you from traveling beyond their limits. They will give you power over your schedule and commitments and help you make future healthy choices.

Simply Simplify

We live in a world of bigger, better, faster, stronger and more. Some would even add "excessive," and while I don't believe there is anything wrong with having some nice things or many nice things, generally speaking more stuff equals more stress. I'm sure each of us could use a little simplicity in our family life. Picture a life less complicated, with clarity and, potentially, easier. Picture your family life with less calendar clutter and activity noise. Breathe in, breathe out, wax on, wax off.

Pardon the phrase here, but simple math would tell you that the more you have, the more you will maintain. If you were to Google "simplify life," a long list of sites would appear, and those wouldn't necessarily include the books, blogs, magazines and movies all geared to help you live life simply. This desire to simply simplify is "generally known as 'voluntary simplicity,' or the 'simplicity movement,' the need many of us see for a less stressful, more meaningful life."[7]

Voluntary simplicity does not mean doing without things entirely or getting rid of everything you have. Voluntary simplicity is a much broader philosophy of living life in a balanced way.

With that in mind, here are seven ways to voluntarily simplify life right now:

1. *Begin screening your calls.* Don't answer the phone just because someone calls you. And if you don't recognize the caller ID, consider not answering the call at all!

2. *Turn off your cell phone.* Does it really need to be on all the time? Can't you (shouldn't you?) turn it off for a couple of hours? Maybe put it on airplane mode. Think baby steps if you can't simply throw the switch.

3. *If you have a cell phone, consider getting rid of your land line.* I haven't answered our home phone in over a year. Why? Because anyone that I want or need to talk to has my cell number. I recently went through the voice messages on our land line, and out of the many, and I do mean many, messages that were left, not one was life threatening, and over 95 percent of the messages were sales calls.

4. *Let voicemail or the answering machine take your calls, especially when you don't want interruptions.* If numbers 1, 2 and 3 are too out there for you, that's okay. Consider a baby step here with number 4. Let the call go to voicemail, and you can respond when you have time to do so.

5. *Answer email twice a day.* Just because someone needs a response "now" doesn't mean you need to respond now. Since I moved to answering email twice a day, I can't tell you how many problems seem to get resolved without my input or advice.

6. *Stop answering all texts immediately.* (I wanted to make sure you were reading and that you hadn't fallen into the "I can't do that" mode.) Pavlov was right. When I hear that alert letting me know I have a text, I start to salivate. We have been programmed to reach for our phones when we hear that sound. Reaching for our phones has become a reflexive—and excessive—way of life. But should it be? In the pilot episode of *Modern Family,* Phil calls for his kids to come downstairs: "Kids,

get down here." One of the children enters the kitchen on her phone and says, "Why are you guys yelling at us? We were way upstairs. Just text me."[8] Yes, texting is a part of life, but it isn't all of life. *Shhh.* Silence your text alert.

7. *Digitize everything.* No more paper. Go green, and put everything into digital files on your computer. Then back everything up in the cloud. No more looking through files that are hanging in those old file drawers. Now you can search for your files using key words, so finding the file you need or want is only a keystroke away.

Although I can't validate the story, urban legend suggests that Albert Einstein's wardrobe consisted only of black pants and white shirts. The reasoning behind the simple wardrobe was that it eliminated having to make choices (an end-to-end principle) every morning. By only having black pants and white shirts, he didn't have to spend any time thinking about what matched what or what pants went with what shirt. His choice of what to wear had already been made for him.

Whether or not you subscribe to Einstein's fashion philosophy—or hairstyle for that matter—isn't the point. The point is to simply simplify life!

2

Plan Moments of Rest

Don't underestimate the value of Doing Nothing, of just going along,
listening to all the things you can't hear, and not bothering.
A. A. MILNE, *POOH'S LITTLE INSTRUCTION BOOK*

I have been challenged with a particular phrase for some time now. A lot of people talk about it, and you have probably said it; and if you were to Google this particular phrase, you would find countless pictures and/or illustrations of it. Articles, books and blogs have been written about it and they all describe the same thing. So I am not in the majority or even the minority on the subject, but right now, I may be the only voice.

The phrase I am talking about is "Work-Life Balance."

When I Googled the phrase, the most common illustration I saw was a picture of a scale with the word "Work" on one side and the word "Life" on the other. I think the picture is at best misleading and at worst wrong.

Let me first start with a couple of definitions of the word "balance." As a verb, "balance" means "to bring to or hold in equilibrium."[1] If you have ever balanced a broom or long stick in your hand, then you have attempted to fulfill this definition. If you have ever watched an elephant in the circus balance on a ball, or a tightrope walker on a line, or a gymnast performing a routine on the balance beam, then you have observed this definition in action.

As a noun, "balance" is "an instrument for determining weight, typically by the equilibrium of a bar with a fulcrum at the center, from each end of which is suspended a scale or pan, one holding an object of known weight, and the other holding the object to be weighed."[2] This definition of balance may be a bit harder to understand since we rarely use such scales to weigh anything today. A balance scale uses a horizontal arm known as a beam attached to a fulcrum at the midpoint of the beam. There is a pan that hangs from each end of the beam. When objects of equal weight are placed into each pan, the scale will balance them. If one item is heavier than the other, it will tilt to that side.

A scale like this was primarily used to compare two different weights and used a standard weight on one side with the unknown weight on the other. For example, if you wanted a pound of flour, then the owner of the flour would put a standard one-pound weight on one end of the balance and then scoop flour and add it to the other side of the scale until equilibrium—one pound of flour—had been measured out. A standard weight on one side and an equal weight on the other and balance was achieved.

Here is the million-dollar question: Which definition of balance is best applied to life balance? I suggest the definition for the noun, and here's why. "Balance" defined as a verb is not sustainable. You can't get an elephant to balance on top of a ball for very long, and even the best gymnast in the country will eventually fall off the beam during a routine. "Balance" defined as a noun is sustainable; we just need to find a standard to place on one side of the scale. So the question is, "What is the standard for balancing life?"

Since I believe the noun definition of "balance" applies to life balance, I would like to suggest a standard to place on one side of the scale. The standard I am thinking of is "time." Think about it: Each one of us has 24 hours in our day, and we each have 7 days in a week. Time is our standard when it comes to life balance. What we place on the other side of the balance scale depends on several things: our age, season of life, roles and responsibilities. These all vary from person to person and family to family, but the bottom line is that you only have 24 hours to get it all done. If you put too much on one side of the scale, you will be out of balance. Likewise, if you don't put enough on the scale, you will be out of balance. One extreme leads to burnout and the other to laziness. The goal is balance.

When we say "work-life balance" and put work on one side of the scale and life on the other, we are saying that either work is the standard and we must balance everything to work, or life is the standard and we must balance work to it. I think we need a paradigm shift. I think we need to change the phrase and let it affect our thinking. We need to move from work-life balance to life-time balance. After all, work is a subset of life, isn't it? Yes, work is a big part of life, but it's still a part of life; it is not life. Family is a part of life; hobbies, friends, extended family, sports, working out, eating, sleeping—all are subsets of life with the standard of measure being time.

If time is our standard, then we need to be aware of what we are putting on the scale for every one of the 24 hours in each day. If you have a family with three children and work a full-time job, your pan is almost full. Let's say it *is* full! Let's say you are working eight hours a day and, in addition, maybe a little overtime when and where you can. Well, if that's true, the scale may start to tip out of balance. To bring life back into balance with your available time, you must either remove something from the life side or put more time, or weight, on the other. Knowing you can't get more time, you will be forced to wrestle with what gets removed from the other side. So what do you do? Remove one of your kids? That would equal out the scale, wouldn't it?

If we had to physically reach into that pan on the life side and remove one thing in order to bring balance to the time side, it would force us to think twice about what we selected. I don't think anybody would reach in and remove one of their children for a week or a day. We would all reach in and remove a work component. However, since we don't view work-life balance as time-life balance, it makes it easier to simply keep working.

Now, I am not asking you to adopt this unconventional view right out of the gate, but allow it to marinate in your soul and see if it doesn't make sense to you and your life situation. If we have no standard in our life, then we can never be in balance, because we don't know what we are trying to be in balance with.

Traditional View   Unconventional View

Too Much of a Good Thing

If you were to ask me what I think the biggest obstacle facing today's modern family is, I would tell you "too many choices." Those choices are rarely between good and bad; they're mostly between good and better. This changes our way of thinking. We say to ourselves, *If one is good, then more must be better*, and that is rarely, if ever, the case.

Parents today are faced with a unique opportunity that's actually too much of a good thing. Twenty years ago, the pace of life was more predictable because our choices were somewhat limited. As far as sports, we could play baseball, football or basketball, and that was it. When we went to a movie, we had two options: the movie playing at theater A or the movie playing at theater B.

My family went to the movies last week, and the same movie was playing in four different theaters: One version of the movie was playing with enhanced RPX sound technology; another version was being shown in 3D; a third option was the IMAX large screen experience; and the fourth option was to see the movie in a normal room on a normal screen with normal sound and a normal experience. But who wants normal?

Who wants to be normal when you can have an amazing experience? Bigger sound, bigger picture, bigger experience, bigger drinks. (Don't get me started on the beverage sizes at the movies.

My bladder couldn't hold what is called a small drink at the local theater.)

And how about TV? Not too many years ago, there were five television channels, and there was no such thing as a remote control. Actually, I was the remote control! My son Alec was standing in front of the TV the other day holding the remote to cycle through channels like an ADD hamster out for a run on its wheel. After a minute of crash-course channel surfing, he tossed the remote on the couch and said, "There's nothing good on."

What? Nothing good on? Was he kidding? I said, "You have a thousand channels!" (The definition of "nothing good on" when I was a kid was five channels and a speech by the president being broadcast—when he was speaking, he was on all five channels at once!)

During my childhood, there were no laptop computers or wireless anything. We had phones with cords on them! Moments of rest tended to come to us more naturally than they do today. Life's pace, though, is viewed by each generation as moving too fast, and each generation struggles with work-life, excuse me, time-life balance.

> Looking out at the road rushing under my wheels
> I don't know how to tell you all just how crazy this life feels
> I look around for the friends that I used to turn to, to pull
>   me through
> Looking into their eyes I see them running too
>   Running on, running on empty.[3]

Before Jackson Browne penned those lyrics for his classic song "Running on Empty" (1977), the nineteenth-century British theologian Frederick William Faber wrote,

> It is very unusual for there to be complete quiet in the soul, for God almost continually whispers to us. And whenever the sounds of the world subside in our soul, we hear the whispering of God. Yes, He continues to whisper to us, but

we often do not hear Him because of the noise and distractions caused by the hurried pace of our life.[4]

And before Faber wrote his words, Solomon said, "I discovered that there is ceaseless activity, day and night" (Eccles. 8:16).

Apparently running on empty, distractions, hurry and ceaseless activity have been a topic for a while. What does this tell
us? Can we really look back a couple of thousand years and say
those people were busy? Did they really have an over-work problem? I would say yes, they did. But I do think there is a difference between their over-work and our over-work. It is true they
had fewer choices and fewer options in life. Their over-work was
done to sustain life. Should I feed the animals today so that my
family can have food tomorrow? After that, should I plant the
field so that my family can have grain for next season? Should
I dig a well so that my family has water? After that, should I go
into town and try to trade or barter some of our vegetables for
things we need?

The choices for over-work 2,000 years ago were different from
our choices today, mostly because of our ability to be constantly connected. You couldn't plow a field at night back then; you
came indoors and rested. Today, after you complete your work,
you can answer email. Welcome to the modern family! Each generation must solve busyness within the context of their world.
However, regardless of what generation we were born and raised
in, over-work comes down to the same thing for each of us: choices.
How are we choosing to invest our time?

The "Am I Too Busy?" Quiz

Here is a 60-second "Am I too busy?" quiz for you to take. Answer
the following 10 questions yes or no and notice how the questions
apply to our modern "need" to hurry. When you're done taking
the quiz, hand the questions to your spouse and/or each of your
children and have them take the quiz about how they see you.

(You can also take the quiz online and see your immediate results by heading over to www.whowillyouempower.com/amitoobusy.)

1. I often commit to things when I don't know how much time or energy it will require.
2. I am always tired and never feel like I've accomplished enough at the end of the day.
3. I seldom schedule a day off for myself, and when I do, I fill it with activities.
4. I have difficulty saying no.
5. I often miscalculate how long certain activities will take.
6. I find myself constantly wishing I had more time.
7. I rarely have time to do the things I really love.
8. I feel powerless over my time and commitments.
9. I rarely, if ever, schedule downtime on my calendar.
10. Others complain that my schedule doesn't allow enough time for them.

If you answered yes to questions 1 through 4, you are on the right track or in complete denial. (My friend Doah tells me, "The problem with denial is that you don't know when you are in it. That's why it's called denial.") Makes sense.

If you answered yes to questions 5 through 7, you are on a path to hectic, not healthy.

If you answered yes to questions 8 through 10, you are too busy.

Although this quiz is in no way a scientific measurement of how busyness affects you individually or as a family, it does ask a few important questions to get you thinking about busyness. Most of us don't need a quiz; we know we are busy, but we don't know why. I will be one of the first to say that busyness isn't what hurts us—it's the stress! Dr. Archibald Hart describes stress this way: "The stress that does us in is the stress of challenge, high energy output and over commitment."[5] "If we do not build enough time into our lives to allow recovery of the system, we pay for it in stress disease."[6]

It used to be that just one member of the family was always work-ing or overdoing. Of course, that had negative effects on the family, but I am not talking about that one person here. I used to be that one person. What I'm talking about is a new kind of busyness—the kind that doesn't just affect one family member but includes every-one in the family.

We parents get up and go to work. Our kids get up and go to school. Then our lives are filled with sports, practices, games, events, meet-ings, small-group activities, large-group get-togethers, this trip, that trip, homework, chores, and, oh, don't forget sleep.

Do the Math

After a back-to-school night for our kids, I did a little math. I added up how much time each teacher expected the students to spend on homework on each subject. Later that week at a parent meeting, the amount of time required to participate in a sport was explained. Much of that time included arriving prior to practice, staying after practice, selling things to raise money for the sport, attending out-side events related to the sport, and helping to represent the team at other events at the school. And of course, how much time (as well as money!) parents were required to volunteer to work the snack bar, take pictures, keep the score sheet, provide snacks—you get the idea.

Disclaimer: I am not saying these things are wrong or bad or unhealthy. I am saying that we simply can't do it all.

Back to the math: After I added up what was expected of our kids, I figured that each of them had 7 hours and 30 minutes of free time.

School	7:30 A.M.–3:00 P.M.
Practice	3:00 P.M.–6:00 P.M.
Homework	6:00 P.M.–12:00 A.M. (6 classes x 1 hour each class)

If you look closely, you will notice that I have not put in travel time, eating or sleeping. Sometimes I feel as if our family is stuck on the hamster wheel. Individual stress has turned into family stress.

We spend so much time going in different directions that stress has become commonplace. And it all seems necessary. If you want your child to go to college, if you want your child to get a scholarship, if you want your child to make the team, if you want your child to excel on the team, if you want your child to . . . you get the idea.

It never really ends, does it? Mary and I are no longer the workaholics in the family. Our kids are! But we as parents have to start thinking differently as parents.

In *Hectic to Healthy,* I ask the question, "Can you say no to an opportunity for yourself that leads to a workaholic lifestyle?" I think there is another question that confronts us today: Can you say no to an opportunity for your children? When you say no to an opportunity for one of your kids, there will be consequences—not for you, but for him or for her.

Do you tell a teacher at school, "Thank you for all you do for my son. We really appreciate your enthusiasm. We did want to let you know, though, that our son will not be doing your assigned homework every evening; he will only do homework for a few minutes every other night. Thanks for understanding."

Do you tell the coach, "Wow, we really appreciate your enthusiasm for creating a winning team. Love the energy! I did want to let you know, though, that we will be taking our daughter out of practice an hour early each day so that our family can have some balance in life. Thanks!"

Know Rest, No Stress

We have a responsibility to our families to find time to rest our bodies, relax our minds, recover our emotions and pursue some recreation to provide our lives with some relief from an overachieving, over-committed lifestyle.

Stress today is much different from stress in previous times in two distinct ways. First, today's stress has increased with our accelerated pace of life. Second, our modern technology has reduced the availability of recovery time.

Work or over-work, doing or overdoing used to be done in chunks of time. Someone who was a workaholic 2,000 years ago would probably work 10 straight hours in the field, and then that person was done. There was a predictable ebb and flow to the life-styles of ancient people. Recall the stories in the book of Exodus, for example. Life had less stuff, fewer choices, less clutter. I'm not saying the Israelites had less stress. But their stress was different from what we experience. They didn't have the capability to be "on," or connected, all the time.

Work or over-work, doing or overdoing now are rarely done in chunks of time; it is an ongoing process. Our personal lives are intertwined with work. Our modern conveniences have allowed this style of living. The Internet, smartphones, tablets, social media—our connectivity—allow us to be on and productive all the time. Doing comes in bursts of productivity throughout the day, not in one or two chunks of time as it did several hundred years ago.

The stress that gets to families today isn't the temporary stress caused by a dramatic life event or difficult crisis. The stress that gets to families is the constant connectivity and compounding over-commitment that comes from an inability to disconnect or unplug from work moments in healthy ways.

Five Steps to Moments of Rest

Obviously, we all need to find some balance and family rest, but let's not focus on the next five years. Let's focus on the next five days. So what can you do over the next five days to instill a little stop into the life of your family?

Step 1: Schedule It

Please stop reading quickly for a moment and digest the next story before checking this chapter off your "I read it" list.

Carey Nieuwhof, a friend of mine, and I were speaking at a conference together, and while we were eating lunch, we started talking about—of all things—our blogs. During the conversation, he asked me if I had read Michael Hyatt's book *Platform*. I said, "Yes, it was a great book!" Carey then asked me, "What have you done that has been most useful to you from reading the book?" Huh? I remembered the book—it was a good book. I still had it on my iPad! What was this nonsense Carey was asking me? Something about doing what I read?

I'm sorry, I'm an idiot. (Wait, positive self-talk.) I behaved like an idiot in that moment. Apparently, there is a difference in the lives of people who read books and call them good and people who read books and put a few things they've read into practice. I used to do the former, but now I am moving to the latter with everything I read. I wanted you to have that story in your mind before moving on to the next numbered point.

In fact, this might be a good stopping point for today's reading. Take a look at Ecclesiastes 4:5-6: "They say that we would be fools to fold our hands and let ourselves starve to death. Maybe so, but it is better to have only a little, with peace of mind, than be busy all the time with both hands, trying to catch the wind" (*GNB*). If you've decided to take a moment here, open up your calendar—it's probably already in your hand or at least nearby—and pick one day in the next week. Block off 30 minutes of time one evening and call it Family Rest. (Don't forget to tell your family about the rest time, and make sure all of you remember to do it.) Now, on to point two (or day two if you decided to stop reading here and think about this point in depth.

Step 2: Say No

I know, easy to say, hard to do. When life gets busy this week, give yourself permission to say no to a few things. You're not saying no forever, just for this week. Say no to a school event, extra practice for one of your children or even a small-group meeting. Use the time to get caught up or just relax. Think of it this way: If you keep saying yes to everything, you are saying no to something by default.

Generally speaking, the more you say yes, the more it leads to stress; the more you say no, the more it leads to slow.

Learning to say no isn't as easy as it seems. It's less of a science and more of an art if you want to be tactful about it. Let's face it, some personalities have a hard time saying no. Mary and I are two of them! We aren't talking about saying no to unimportant things. We are talking about saying no to good things, even great things. How about saying no to an additional opportunity to serve at church when you are already plugged in to serving on a weekly basis? We are not suggesting saying no to serving; we are suggesting that you say no to an addiction to serving. Each of us is called to help, volunteer and make a difference in the lives of others. So serve! Do it! Just don't overdo it.

When serving others causes us to consistently neglect our families, then we have a problem. Signing up for every opportunity that comes our way, without a thought of the cost it will have on our families, is unhealthy.

Sometimes the reason it's so difficult to say no to overdoing is that the things we are being asked to do or get involved with are not just good, worthwhile and compelling things, they are great things! When someone asks me to do something or volunteer for something, I find myself just saying yes without knowing what I'm doing. It's almost a reflex. I have heard people say, "I would rather burn out than rust out." I probably would have agreed with that at one time; but I can tell you from personal experience learned in crisis, you can't do it all.

So how do you actually say no? The art of saying no is different for each person, for each family. As mentioned earlier, a healthy yes for your family could be an unhealthy no for another family. And there's an added dilemma: What do you do when the person who has approached you to give your time to a project or cause has the charisma of a movie star and the passion of a motivational speaker? And what if the person is asking not only for a good cause but a great one! How do you say no in that moment? Here are a few thoughts.

Take Some Time

When someone asks you to do something, you don't need to give an immediate answer. Take some time to pray about it. Consider your calendar and the time commitment it will take, as well as how it will affect your family. If the person wants an immediate answer, then it's a no.

When our kids were younger, they had a habit of putting us on the spot when asking if a friend could have a sleep-over. We have always told our kids that if they put us in a difficult situation or put us on the spot in front of others, the answer will always be no. This applies to the occasional requests from our teenagers that come from the backseat of the car as we are driving. My standard default statement is, "Mom and I need to process that first." (As a parent, you know you can't always give a yes or no answer without talking it over.) If during the drive the kids continue to ask, the response is always, "Do you want an answer right now?" "No, no. Please, no." Our kids have learned that if they want my answer right now, the answer will always be no.

Talk It Over

Have a conversation with your spouse and agree on a decision together. Occasionally, and more often now that our kids are older, we will ask their opinion on certain things and get their feedback as well. All of us are smarter than one of us.

Be Polite

There is no reason for being rude when you have to say no to someone. Let me give you an example.

> Question: "Hey, Craig, we have a mission trip coming up.
>   A few of us were talking, and we think you would be
>   perfect to lead the group. What do you think?"
> Answer: "NO!"

Harsh, right? Let's try it again.

> Question: "Hey, Craig, we have a mission trip coming up. A few of us were talking, and we think you would be perfect to lead the group. What do you think?"
>
> Answer: "Wow! Thanks for considering me. I would love to go. Mission trips are really part of who I am. Unfortunately, I can't lead this time, but please ask me again in the future. I would love to help when I can."

Both answers were a no, but the second one was presented with respect and consideration.

Step 3: Plan Ahead

I'm not a planner, but my wife, Mary, is. She is amazingly organized and calendar oriented. Each Sunday we sit down for a few minutes of undivided, undistracted attention and walk through each day of the following week, making sure we are both on the same page. We talk about when our kids have practices, when they have a game, who is taking them and who is picking them up. We talk about when small group is for our kids and for us. We talk about when we are eating together as a family that particular week and even what we are having for dinner. Plan it, calendar it, balance it, do it.

Step 5: Don't Worry

If you are thinking to yourself, *Why didn't Craig or the folks at Regal catch that typo in the numbering order; that really bothers me,* then you may have an opportunity to work on worry, control or perfectionism. Sometimes you just need to let stuff go. Worry isn't productive. If you don't believe me, listen to what Solomon and Paul have to say about worry:

> Worry weighs a person down; an encouraging word cheers a person up (Prov. 12:25).

Don't worry about anything; instead, pray about every-thing. Tell God what you need, and thank him for all he has done (Phil. 4:6).

Step 4: Smarter Not Harder

Just because we have the ability to be connected 24-7 doesn't mean we should always be connected, but we should embrace modern technology and use it to our advantage. Modern technology allows us to accomplish more things in less time and, very often, with less effort. Think of paying bills. Before paying online was available, you would receive a paper bill in the mail, open it, pull out the statement, find your checkbook, write a check, tear off the part of the bill you were supposed to return with the payment, seal it in a return envelope, buy a stamp and put it in the mailbox.

Before writing that paragraph, I paid seven bills from one screen in three minutes—no stamp, no check, no mailbox—and it synched to my checking software and balanced my checkbook with a click of a button. We should use what we can to work smarter, not hard-er. "Using a dull ax requires great strength, so sharpen the blade. That's the value of wisdom; it helps you succeed" (Eccles. 10:10).

Just remember, after you use the technology, unplug for a while so you can provide those necessary moments of rest for your entire family.

3

Schedule Uninterrupted Time Together

I think time management as a label encourages people to view each 24-hour period as a slot in which they should pack as much as possible.
TIM FERRISS

Do you like a good sale? You know, the "take 50 percent off the already low price" kind of a sale! Love those. You get quality merchandise at a great value. I guess if I have one complaint about such a sale it's that they usually don't last beyond a week at the most. If you don't make time now—while the sale is on—then you will have missed a great opportunity.

We are reminded to take advantage of a good sale or good opportunity in the Bible. It's true! Ephesians 5:15-17 talks all about it:

> So be careful how you live. Don't live like fools, but like those who are wise. Make the most of every opportunity in these evil days. Don't act thoughtlessly, but understand what the Lord wants you to do.

Now, you may be inclined to take the words "what the Lord wants you to do" as an instruction to go and take advantage of every great sale at the mall. I would say A for effort, but that's not the part of these verses that talks about a sale. It's actually the words "make the most of every opportunity." Those six words literally mean "buying the time." Now, we all know there isn't a place that sells time, so what does it mean to "buy the time"? The thought goes back centuries and was a metaphor taken from the time when merchants would observe the best time to sell their goods, much like ads for a sale catch our attention today.

A few years ago, I was invited to be a guest speaker on a cruise ship. As it turned out, I was available! When the ship arrived at our first port of call, passengers had the option of staying on the ship or disembarking and walking around town. We opted for the second. Once we stepped off the ship, we were met by at least 50 people selling T-shirts, jewelry, purses and food. I guess you could say they were in the right place at the right time. Pretty smart to be in that exact location at the very moment when the ship arrived. It's like they somehow knew. Well, of course they knew, and I'm sure they knew when the next ship was due into the port as well. You see, they were "buying the time"—taking advantage of the opportunity.

Just as a modern sale has a beginning and an end, and just as our cruise had specific arrival and departure times, so too our time on earth is limited, and we need to be ready to take advantage of the time we have. To put it bluntly, our children sail into our lives and then sail out. We have a limited time with them, so we must take advantage of the opportunity. We must buy the time we have with them now. We can't just sit back and expect all the good deals in life to come to us. We must do the looking and comparing to find the best way to make the most of our time with our family. That will mean saying no to some good opportunities in favor of better opportunities, or the best opportunity.

We can only do this by reaching forward and looking ahead. When we look back and see what we have missed, we may say, "Now that I look back, I should have taken advantage of that opportunity." Our hindsight is pretty clear. It's when we look ahead that life can appear to be a little fuzzy; but that's where our faith comes in. We ask God for the wisdom necessary to make the most of our time, and we take advantage of every opportunity we have with our family. If we don't take advantage of our time, it will sail away; it will pass us by. Time does not stop while we try to decide how to best take advantage of it. Time is relentless that way. Taking advantage of each opportunity requires a certain diligence and planning from each one of us.

You Need All Three

Every day while picking up my kids at school, I experience organized chaos. For those of you who do a little picking up yourself, you know what I am talking about. From my general observation of all the parents who pick up their kids, myself included, I find that the parents fall into one of three types: (1) parents who watch life happen, (2) parents who let life happen, and (3) parents who make life happen. To be honest, no one type is better than the others—there isn't a right or a wrong way to react; we're all just different. Let me explain.

1. Parents Who Watch Life Happen

These parents pick up their kids and pull over. They sit, watch and wait until all traffic has cleared. It's not that they don't have a desire to move; they just don't have a desire to move now. They wait until it's less congested. They are polite and usually courteous. They don't hold up the line; they're simply not in a rush. They are content to sit and watch life happen.

2. Parents Who Let Life Happen

These parents get their kids in the car and then let circumstances dictate their position. They stay in line but make no effort to inch out into traffic. They make no attempt to create a small opportunity for someone to "wave them in." They will sit with their foot on the brake until the right time comes.

3. Parents Who Make Life Happen

These parents are assertive but not aggressive; they are aware but not obsessed. They understand that if they don't take a small opportunity to inch forward into traffic, they will never get into the flow. They take the initiative to make it happen and keep moving forward.

Depending on your personality, I'm sure you have already identified with one of the above parking-lot parents. As a higher-strung parent, I immediately gravitate to the group of parents who make life happen; but the reality is that all three types of these parenting personalities are important in your parenting style, depending on the time and circumstance. In fact, you need to be all three styles when it comes to scheduling uninterrupted time together with your family.

Combining the Three Parent Types

To schedule uninterrupted time, you will need to start as a parent who makes life happen, especially if you have more than one child and they are all teenagers. It will take some assertiveness to get something on the calendar. Spending uninterrupted time together will also involve your watching life happen. Sitting by once you are all together and hearing those first few words from your beautiful children, "This is boring . . . why are we doing this . . . why can't we have our phones" or anything else that may verbally roll down the hill will be an exercise in patience and waiting for the congestion to move.

Finally, you will need to exhibit that let-it-happen component. You can't force it. You can't inch out into family traffic. You must sit with your foot on the verbal brake and see what happens. Even those parents who "let it happen" in the parking lot eventually start moving after everyone has left. You may just need to wait it out and let a little traffic clear.

Practicing the Three Parent Types

Let me tell you about how Mary and I recently put into practice being the three types of parent in one. As an uninterrupted time together, we had scheduled a hike to Holy Jim Falls, not too far from our home here in Southern California. We told our kids that we were going to take a hike after church. "Seriously? Why? How far? Do we get cell reception?" We pretty much expected a few such responses, but oddly, we didn't receive any of those. There was some general reluctance, but overall the kids were neutral about the hike. We drove to the trailhead, got out and started walking. Yes! We made life happen!

During our hike, I misread a sign and instead of a two-mile hike, it was a bit longer (no need to relive that here in this book). There was some general conversation about how long the hike would now take and when we would return home. There was an event they were supposed to go to and were looking forward to as well. With the added time and a few off-the-path explorations by the three Jutila boys (me included), the hike took much longer than we had expected. So we were faced with a choice: Do we rush out to make the deadline for the next event or do we let our time together on the hike run its course?

We could have made a good case for either of our options. Hustling out could be fun, and we did have something else on the calendar. But not having to watch the clock and just hanging out with the family had its advantages too. There wasn't a consensus on what we should do. Mary and I were up for either option. One of our kids wanted to explore, one wanted to hurry back, and one didn't care. So we opted for option two and just let life happen—we moved the hike along but didn't rush it. In fact, as we were driving out, we even stopped to record a tarantula that Mary saw crossing the road. It was awesome!

As we were driving home, we watched life happen. Our kids kept asking what we were going to do. Were we going to make the next event? Mary and I didn't answer. We wanted to see what they would do, how they would respond. It became obvious that time was not on our side when we were still on the road at 7:30, the exact time the other event was starting. Reality set in and the kids had their answer. "We're not going to make the other event, are we?" I said, "I don't think we are. Why don't we just go home and have some dinner and hang out, maybe watch a movie?" Everyone agreed and we headed home.

I admit that it's hard for me to watch life happen when I already know what I want to happen. But it's not about what I want; it's about what we want as a family. A family vision statement and a list of family values (which I will talk about in the last part of this book) will help when it comes to making decisions; but regardless of your priorities, everything can't be neatly and quickly decided all the time. Making life happen, letting it happen and watching it happen all come into play when spending uninterrupted time together as a family.

Please Do Not Disturb

When I make an attempt to spend uninterrupted time with my family, I feel as if I am fighting constant distractions and interruptions. The bling, hum or alarm from a text or social media app is certainly distracting; but even if I am in a location that's quiet and with no cell reception, I find myself battling my overactive brain, which never seems to shut down (probably because it has gotten used to the way the Internet wants us to think in rapid, bit-sized chunks of information). The bottom line is that I need to stop interrupting myself before I can spend uninterrupted time with my family.

After getting myself unplugged, the next challenge is getting the rest of the family to unplug. Our kids are pretty good about unplugging when we have calendared family time, including doing a pretty good job of respecting the family boundary of no electronics at the dinner table. We want our times together to engage our kids—to have a conversation and connect with them.

Unplugging is not really a modern family problem though. I can remember when I was younger. I had a hand-held video football game. It's probably better described as a box that fit in your hand with six buttons and a bunch of blips that looked like a minus sign or hyphen. I would play that game every chance I got. I remember playing it in the car when I would take trips with my grandparents.

We would be driving by an amazing river or beach and my grandpa would say, "Put down that game and look around you. There are some amazing things to see. Look out the window." I would glance out the window, make a comment, "Yeah, cool," and then go back to the game.

I want our family times to be different. Of course there are times when it's okay to play on your phone during a long drive or listen to music or send a message to a friend. I just don't want my kids to isolate themselves every time they get in the car. The same is true for Mary and me. If we want to connect with our kids while in the car, we can't be on our phones talking to others. We need to simply unplug and be present so we can relationally connect with our kids.

I am not suggesting your family should sit, stand, retreat or isolate themselves in order to have uninterrupted time together. Spending uninterrupted time together may involve something such as a walk, a car ride or even a video game (if it's one you can take turns playing). The point is that you spend uninterrupted time together—"together" being the operative word. One of the things we like to do as a family is watch a TV series together. Every Tuesday night we sit down together, eat some popcorn (although I am partial to my wife's brownies), and watch the show. For our family, in that hour, there are no interruptions. The TV is not an interruption for us. In this case, it's what brings us together. We talk, make comments and sometimes back up the program to watch something we missed. We are connecting with each other, with no phones in the room and nothing to distract us.

If you want to spend some uninterrupted time together, then you need to make sure that each person in your family, parents and children, is disconnected from whatever media they use. Technology doesn't have to interfere with your family's uninterrupted time. In fact, technology can enhance it. But each family member should not be connected to his or her own channel. If you are having a family TV night but your kids want to text, play a game, read a book, or post something on a social media site that's not relevant to what you are doing together, have them turn it off. They need to plug in to the rest of the family. They will have plenty of time to do something else at a different time. Right now is family time.

Good, Better, Best

I think there are three general options when it comes to spending uninterrupted time together. There are good options, better options and best options. If you can't do best, then try better; and if better doesn't work, go with good.

Our family's spending every Tuesday night watching a TV show together is a good option for us. I have ideas of what is better and what is best; but on Tuesday night at 8:00 P.M.—after homework, dinner and any practices are over—watching a television show is a good option for us.

The best option would be to go for a walk on the beach together, exploring tide pools, with cell phones and all things media left at home or in the car—disconnected and unreachable from the frenetic world, but reachable and connected as a family. Unplugged, so to speak. I wish we could do that all the time. It would be in the "best option" category for me. However, best isn't always available, so we plan for good.

Think about your options and discuss them with your spouse and then with your family. Determine what would be a good option, what would be a better option and what would be the best option. Then decide which will work for your family to keep you reachable and connected to each other, and go with that option.

Three Steps to Uninterrupted Time Together

1. Calendar It

There seems to be one thing in particular that illustrates the least amount of simplicity and clarity about getting family time coordinated: the family calendar! I have seen everything used from a piece of paper on the refrigerator—one piece of paper for each person in the family—to a digital calendar kept in the cloud and maintained by each family member on his or her own separate device. And some family members don't participate; three people in the family maintain separate calendars while two others do not calendar anything at all! Whether you prefer a calendar in the cloud or a calendar in the kitchen, the key is to calendar your family time. With that in mind, let's take a quick look at getting everyone on the same page, or in this case, on the same calendar.

There are several free calendar programs available online. I tossed a question out on Facebook asking if parents use a family calendar system and, if so, which one. From the responses I received, most families, 10 to 1, are using digital calendars to manage and plan their family's schedule. The top three calendars that were being used by the parents who responded were Google Calendar,[1] iCal,[2] and Cozi,[3] in that order. All of our family is on Apple's OS, so using iCal is the best answer for us.

The bottom line is to do what works for you and your family. However, I would like to make a suggestion to at least explore a few digital options for calendaring your family time. There are several benefits to using online calendars. Here are my top five reasons to go digital.

Reason Number 1: You Will Never Lose It

I know, never say never, right? There is always that one instance when someone loses his or her calendar online. However, with digital backups, Dropbox and cloud servers, the chances that a digital calendar will be lost forever are slim to none. However, if you lose your paper calendar, it's lost for good.

Reason Number 2: You Can Print It

If you start with a digital calendar, you can always print what you have scheduled if you need to see it on paper or post it on the refrigerator. Any changes that you need to make can be entered on your digital calendar, and then the calendar can be reprinted.

Reason Number 3: You Can See It All . . . or Not

We have five individual calendars within one main calendar. We can see each family member's schedule individually or we can merge them to see everyone's schedule on a master calendar. Each click of the button can change the view from all kids to just mom and dad. One-button ease of use is huge for managing a family whose members have different schedules.

Reason Number 4: You Can Change the View

The calendar can be changed so that a single day, a week, a month, or an entire year can be viewed. With so much coming at a family on a daily basis, it's helpful to be able to look at varying lengths of time for those plans that need to be made well head of time.

Reason Number 5: Everyone Can See It

As parents, it's great to have the digital reins to the master family calendar. In a quick click of a button, we can share appointments and family events, block off uninterrupted family time together, and push those notifications and events to our kids' calendars on their phones. Just make sure your kids understand that they must periodically check their calendars for changes and updates.

Here is a brief mom-daughter conversation on calendaring in our house:

Karimy: "I didn't know we were going to . . ."
Mary: "Did you check your calendar?"
Karimy: "I did, but there isn't anything on my calendar."
Mary: "Check again."
Karimy: "Oh, yeah, I see it."

Once you put everyone's schedule on one calendar, you will begin to see when uninterrupted family times together can be put on the schedule and what, if anything, needs to be removed to allow for those times. This may not be an easy thing to do, but start by deciding the answers to two questions. First, what is most important to you and your family right now? (Dinner together? Game night? Eating out? Family fun night?) Whatever that is, put it on your calendar first because whatever gets scheduled usually gets done. Second, what can you eliminate or stop doing right now? This is probably the more difficult of the two questions because someone in the family usually ends up sacrificing more than someone else, but sacrifice is always a difficult but necessary step in order to move toward simplifying life.

The bottom line is that you have to schedule uninterrupted family times together, and you need to schedule those times in a way that works for your family—be it on a paper calendar or a digital one.

2. Plan It

"It is a commonplace observation that work expands so as to fill the time available for its completion."[4] The preceding quote comes from Cyril Northcote Parkinson and has since come to be known as Parkinson's Law. What Parkinson meant is that two people charged with doing the same thing will each take the amount of time they are given to accomplish the task: One person given 30 minutes to do a job will take 30 minutes to do the job; another person given 90 minutes to do the same job will take 90 minutes to finish the task. Work simply expands to the time allowed to accomplish it.

Let me give you a personal example. I find that I am most productive right before I leave for vacation. The reason for this is that I know I will be away for an extended period of time and I need to get things finished or at least in place so that they keep moving while I'm gone. So I get a lot accomplished in a short amount of time because I only have a short amount of time to finish what needs to be done.

Here's a week's worth of ideas to help you start planning the time:

- Monday: Invite each family member to tell one thing he or she can stop doing to have a better family life pace.

- Tuesday: Just before bedtime, read aloud Ephesians 5:15-16 together as a family; then pray this prayer: "God, help us to be careful with our time. Give us wisdom as a family to know how to make the best use of our time together. Amen."
- Wednesday: Have dinner together and ask each family member, "What were your highs and lows today?"
- Thursday: Write a separate note to each of your children, letting each child know how much you love him or her. Include the note in each child's lunch, or post each note on the mirror in the bathroom for each child to see.
- Friday: Collect each family member's phone and put the phones in a drawer. Spend the next hour playing a board game that gets you all talking.
- Saturday: As a family, look ahead on your calendar and find a block of time that is at least four hours long. Label the block "Family Time" and block the entire time. Then vote to decide what you will do during that time together.
- Sunday: Ask each family member, "What one thing can we start doing as a family next week to give us uninterrupted time together?"

3. Unplug It

I have heard them called power outlets, power bars, power strips, extension blocks and surge protectors. Each surge protector in my office has six outlets. I have two surge protectors plugged into the two wall outlets here in my office. I honestly don't use the surge protectors to protect my electronics from some unknown electrical "surge." Truth be told, I use them to give me more outlets so that I can plug more things in! Now, instead of the standard 2 outlets, I have 12. If some is good, then more must be better, right?

It's important for you to have that picture in your mind as I explain the next step of my insanity. There have been a few times in my life when I have added a surge protector to a surge protector.

I know, right? Connecting devices in a series each plugged into each other from one power source is called daisy-chaining (or stupid). The reason behind daisy-chaining is to multiply the usefulness of whatever is on the chain—in my case, the outlets. While the surge protector under my desk seems to be handling the load of what is currently plugged in, I wonder what would happen if I added 20 more? I'm just thinking out loud here, but I may have an overload situation.

A general contractor who is a good friend of mine told me that if I continue to plug surge protectors into surge protectors, I will eventually overload the circuit, which will cause the breaker to pop or blow a fuse. I have found a few similarities between daisy-chaining surge protectors in my office and daisy-chaining activities in my family's life. I mistakenly think that we have unlimited power and that I can continue to plug activities in; but the reality is that if I overload the system, something will pop and the power—the connection—will be lost.

I mistakenly reason that as long as I have an open outlet, I can plug another surge protector into it, giving me six more options (there is that too-many-options issue again). It's the proverbial genie in the bottle. You rub the lamp, out comes the genie, you get three wishes, you burn your first two and for the third you wish for three more wishes! Unlimited, unending, unceasing options. Personally, I find it's easier for me to plug in, connect and ask for three more wishes. It's very difficult for me to unplug, remove and disconnect from the responsibilities I have or things I want.

Calendar it! Sure, why not? That's pretty easy. Find some available time and block it out? Done. Plan it! Of course, it feels like second nature to me. Unplug it? That's the difficult one.

So, how do you unplug? How do you know what to unplug from? Do you unplug from some of the responsibilities at the office? Do you unplug from some of the responsibilities at home? If so, then how do you know which ones to unplug from? And once you figure out what should be unplugged, then what? Then the "calm, focused, undistracted, linear mind [is] pushed aside by a new kind of mind that wants and needs to take in and dole out information in short, disjointed, often overlapping bursts—the faster, the better."[5]

My mind expects short bursts and constant small bytes of information. How do I stay calmly focused and engaged with my family in a world that has given me fast food, Stop-N-Go, phones without cords, instant messaging, only 160 characters or less to tweet, and shampoo and conditioner in the same bottle? My thinking has changed; my mind has been remapped. If I go too long without my iPhone I get the shakes and show symptoms of withdrawal. How do I slip back to being present in the moment? How do I focus on my family without being distracted by what's going on around me?

There are times when my family has attempted to have an uninterrupted time together and has won on all fronts—except that one area that's hardest to manage, ourselves. Even when we are together, my mind seems to run elsewhere. Someone will start to tell me a story, but something catches my eye, so I glance away from the storyteller, letting him or her know I've already lost interest in the story—and the teller. And I'm not alone. With so many things competing for our focus, we have learned to be distracted as if it's now part of us, wired into our DNA. I guess that's why I so relate to the story of Mary and Martha, especially Martha.

Hire Martha but Be Mary

It's easy to armchair quarterback the story of Mary and Martha when you're seated in a Starbucks, sipping a nonfat caramel macchiato while reading an online commentary, drawing obvious conclusions about Martha's ignorance and relentless hurry while Jesus was sitting in her living room. But there is something about Martha's behavior that connects with me. I identify with her personality and driven spirit because it's not my nature to sit and listen and totally unplug. I admire Martha's personality and her ability to get things done. Let me put Mary and Martha in a few different situations, and maybe you'll relate to Martha as well.

It's the biggest game of the season. It's fourth and one, you're on the opponent's 20-yard line with 17 seconds left in the game, and you're down by 6. Mary and Martha are set in the backfield and are both competent and capable of running the football and gaining that precious 1 yard to keep your team's championship hopes alive. As a quarterback in the huddle, are you going to give the ball to Mary or Martha? Me too. Every time. Martha would get the carry.

Football not your sport? No problem. Imagine that there are three seconds left in the state championship basketball game. The team you're coaching is down by one point and you send out your two best-shooting guards, Mary and Martha, out onto the floor. The team has one pass and one chance to shoot. You're familiar with Martha's go-get-'em attitude, while Mary has a tendency to take some time to set up the shot. Who do you want shooting the basketball as time expires? Martha, right?

Okay, sports aren't your thing; I understand. You have been planning a large fall kickoff event at your church. It has taken you 11 months to create a theme, cast the vision, plan the event and publicize it. The clock is ticking as you are just four days away from the event you have worked so hard on for the past year. With many intangibles, errands and loose ends that need to be accomplished prior to the event, your key volunteer leader has to back out because of a family emergency. She has left you with a somewhat organized folder about things you thought had been handled but, in fact, were not. As you sit at your desk and feel a panic attack looming, what begins to run through your mind after you calm down?

You recall that new family that recently started attending your church. You have seen them in the lobby, foyer, narthex . . . that area before you walk into the worship center, church, sanctuary. You know the family, and more importantly, you remember the face of the mom in that family. You have met her a few times.

She is always well put together, her kids always look great and are respectful, her husband . . . is there. Yes, that gal. She appears organized, seems well spoken and, most of all, she can multitask! As a leader yourself, you can spot another leader from a mile away. You rummage through the database to find the family and there's the name, Martha Stevens!

After reading her brief résumé filled in on the new visitor card a few months ago, you realize this is the one to help you. She not only has the skills to accomplish a large event in a short amount of time, but also she has written a book on it! As you start to dial Martha's cell phone to give her the blessed news, there is a knock on your closed office door. "Who is it?" you ask.

"It's Mary Ralston." You know Mary; you have worked with Mary. You have drawn some general conclusions on her work ethic. However, you stop dialing and welcome her in. Mary finds her way to a chair in your office. After a few minutes of small talk, Mary lets you know that she has heard about the recent vacancy in the lead volunteer position for your large event and she is willing to take over where things were left off.

With your hand still touching the phone to dial Martha's number, how do you respond? Do you hand Mary the folder and say, "Have at it, dear"? Or do you pause? Do you craft a response that lets her know she is valued but also lets you off the hook? You could definitely use her help, but maybe you need to "pray" about it. Do you tell her you need to "make a few calls" so you can see if you can get someone else that would be a better fit for the job? What would you do? Well, I can tell you what I would do. I would call Martha and ask her to help.

Why a Martha Deserves the Job
Forgive me here, but I admire Martha's qualities. She was driven, took ownership for what she was responsible for, was a hard worker and had an eye for excellence. She was a born leader. Take a look at what Martha brought to the table (no pun intended).

1. Driven

Martha was a get-it-done person. Something inside of Martha was driving her: driven to be the best, driven to succeed, driven to please, driven to provide for her guest. I'm not sure what was driving her, but most likely it was several things and, no, not all of them were bad; in fact, most of them were good. I don't think she wanted to upset Jesus; in fact, I would say quite the contrary. She wanted to please Him by not just doing what she was good at but also by doing what she was best at—and that was doing!

2. Took Ownership

Martha took pride in and ownership of what she was doing. The story tells us that when Jesus came to this village, "a woman named Martha welcomed Him into her home" (Luke 10:38). It was almost certain that the home where this story took place was Martha's, because the verse says that Martha did the welcoming of Jesus into the home, and it was usually the owner of the home who would welcome a guest at the front door. If this was Martha's home and not Mary's, Martha would take pride in having it clean for her guests, and it would be her responsibility to make sure her guests felt comfortable and to provide them with the absolute best. And for her guests on this day, she probably wanted everything to be extra special. Can you imagine the added pressure she must have felt?

3. Hardworking

Martha was a hard worker. Hard workers who can do many things at once are called multitaskers. Martha was a classic one. A valuable asset when planning an event or project, a hardworking multitasker has the ability to do many things at once and do all of them well. Today's large corporations look for Marthas to hire.

4. Prized Excellence

Martha strove for excellence. I'm not sure someone who prized mediocrity would have rolled out the red carpet for a dinner guest.

No, Martha put it in gear and went to work doing what she could, as fast as she could, the best that she could. I admire that. Those who strive for excellence have a hard time accepting results that are simply good enough, and Martha was no different.

5. A Born Leader

Martha was a leader. In this short narrative described by Luke, we see her welcoming her guest and then preparing for her guest. And although it's not recorded that she asked her sister, Mary, for some help in the kitchen, I believe she did. Well, maybe she didn't ask for help, but maybe she *told* her sister to help. How many of us have moved from a question to a directive because we felt pressure to get something done? Sometimes, naturally gifted leaders get the two mixed up.

Martha was driven to make a difference and took ownership of what she was doing. She was a hard worker who valued excellence as a leader. Now, if you read those characteristics on a résumé, wouldn't you want to hire that person? Me too. These are the qualities we look for when choosing team members and hiring staff. We admire these qualities, and strive for them ourselves, and why not? They are noble traits and valuable characteristics of a leader. So, why did Martha miss it in this narrative?

Why Mary Gets the Prize

The reason why Martha missed getting the "prize" is the same reason why I miss it, why parents miss it, and why most leaders who possess these qualities miss it. They couldn't, in the moment, unplug it. Content to daisy-chain, Martha missed the moment to be fully present and engaged with Jesus. I don't think Martha really wanted to be doing it all. She did want help. But she put the work over the person, the doing over the being. We call that choosing our priorities. Usually, we default to what comes naturally to us, what's easiest for us. For some, sitting at the Master's feet and being fully present comes naturally. For others, working for the

Master and multitasking comes naturally. So, who's right? In this story, in this moment, Mary gets it right. She "unplugged it" and sat at the Lord's feet while Martha kept adding outlets.

After welcoming Jesus into her home, Martha plugged in and got busy in her kitchen. Mary unplugged and sat at Jesus' feet. Mary sat; Martha multitasked. Absorb that moment. Mary . . . sitting. Martha . . . multitasking. Mary sitting . . . Martha multitasking. Let it build for a few minutes. Because what happens next is fairly predictable, and here's why. When you have someone who likes work, loves work, likes doing, loves doing, and they are in the presence of those who can easily unplug, there is great potential for a problem to arise.

The haunting nightmare of the multitasker is spotting non-multitasking people across the room. Such was the case with Martha. Verse 39 tells us that "her sister, Mary, sat at the Lord's feet, listening to what he taught." Yes, she sat. Can you believe it?

Let me go out on a limb here and guess what Martha was thinking: *Lazy, no-good younger sister. She never helps. Typical slacker. This is soooo who she is. Once again, I'm left to get it all done. Honestly, I can't believe Jesus is just sitting in there and not addressing this issue with her.* Have you ever felt that way about someone? Me neither. JK (just kidding). Imagine, though, being busy and working your fingers to the bone to prepare for something of great significance, and there are people in the near vicinity, but they do not even offer to help! I'm sure when you find yourself in a situation like that, you easily keep your attitude and words in check, right? Martha, however, did not.

I can imagine Martha's face as she looked around the corner of the kitchen with her apron on and mixing bowl under her arm. The soup on the stove had started to boil at the same time as her attitude. Sweating, stirring and standing, she blew back into place that piece of hair that had flopped over the front of her face to gently rest on the bridge of her nose, all the while staring at her sister sitting in the living room. "Martha was distracted by the big dinner she was preparing" (Luke 10:40). The key word being "distracted."

I like how dictionary.com defines "distracted": "rendered incapable of behaving, reacting, etc., in a normal manner."[6] Such was Martha's case, in this moment. Let's not forget that Martha's motives were pure. Her desire was to prepare and provide for Jesus, but she let her busyness and anxiety affect her emotions, and out-of-control emotions make smart people stupid. She was plugged in to too many outlets; her circuits were overloaded—and it showed. In fact, it was written all over her face.

If you take a deeper look at the word "distracted," it has an interesting word picture associated with it. The word is translated from the Greek verb *perispa* , meaning "to draw around . . . [as in] women whose faces are literally drawn round with anxiety, with a permanent twist, distracted in mind and in looks."[7] Have you ever heard the expression, "They wear their emotions on their sleeve"? This was one of those times for Martha.

Martha was so distracted by what she was doing and how much needed to be done that her face reflected her attitude. Her face was painted with a permanent twist. She was frustrated and frantically looking for more outlets. When her circuit breaker reached its breaking point, Martha went to Jesus and said, "Lord, doesn't it seem unfair to you that my sister just sits here while I do all the work? Tell her to come and help me" (Luke 10:40).

Why did Martha say this to Jesus? Maybe it was because Mary had ignored Martha when Martha asked her to help. Maybe Martha figured that Mary should have realized that her help was needed and shouldn't have had to be asked, but she was being stubborn or defiant, or maybe she just didn't care. Now, I don't think Martha was really asking Jesus if the situation was fair or unfair. I think Martha assumed that Jesus knew it was unfair, and she wanted Him to acknowledge it in front of Mary so she (Martha) could have the "I told you so" moment backed by God Himself. But she didn't get it.

Have you ever watched a football game that had an amazing ending? Your team goes for it and the running back breaks through the line and runs in for a touchdown as time expires. Powerful!

Maybe you are at a basketball game and your team is down by one point with three seconds left. The ball is given to one of your best shooters and, swish! Game over, you win! The place goes wild! Maybe it's a musical moment where the song builds to a final harmony where all parts ignite into an amazing crescendo that leaves you with goose bumps. If you have ever experienced a crescendo moment of this magnitude, then you can get a feeling of what it was like when Martha "came" to Jesus.

With all the energy of an amazing sports moment or powerful song, Martha's inward anxiety turned to outward agitation and she burst in on Jesus. Martha had become so plugged in to her doing that she entirely forgot her being. I get that way with my family sometimes; do you? Distractions become a way of life, not momentary interruptions. It's as if I am hardwired into busy instead of plugged in to it.

If I had been in Martha's situation, I probably would have said something like, "Hey, Jesus, do you see what's going on here? I am working like a nut to provide a nice dinner, and my sister is just sitting there like a bump on a log. Which, by the way, isn't out of the ordinary for her. I mean, she doesn't ever offer to help me. How rude is that? And, though I didn't want to bring this up, this has been an ongoing conversation since we were old enough to remember. So maybe You can help here. Maybe You can get through to her. You know how I've tried. Maybe You can speak some truth into her life. Can You please tell her to get off her lazy rear and help me out? I know that if You say something, she will do it for once in her life."

Why a Good Intention Isn't Always Good

The road to making a difference in this world is often paved with good, if not great, intentions, not bad ones. Occasionally, though, good intentions can become a stumbling block that trips us up. Think about Martha's intent:

- Was Martha doing something worthwhile? Yes.
- Was Martha's intent to honor Jesus? Yes.

- Was Martha trying to provide a comfortable environment for her guest? Yes.
- Was Martha working hard to prepare something special for someone special? Yes.
- Was Martha trying to be kind and loving? Yes.

I believe Martha was really doing the best she could to provide an amazing, wonderful, warm welcome for Jesus, but her good intention caused her to become so preoccupied with her purpose that she forgot to pause in that moment. It wasn't Martha's intention that tripped her up; it was that she was distracted by it. So she ended up blundering into where Jesus was and blurted out words that she later probably wanted to take back.

While we always look at Martha as the one who was wrong in this situation, she was simply plugged in when she should have unplugged. Sometimes our greatest strength can become our greatest weakness, and the difference is where the line is. Martha's positive leadership qualities had become her weakness in that moment. Despite Martha's good intention, she was consumed with her work, distracted by the details and preoccupied with performance.

What One Thing Matters

Jesus knew the problem Martha had, so He said to her, "My dear Martha, you are worried and upset over all these details. There is only one thing worth being concerned about. Mary has discovered it, and it will not be taken away from her" (Luke 10:41-42).

What is the "one thing" Jesus is talking about here? Some scholars believe the one thing is love. There is only one thing worth being concerned about here, and that one thing is love—who do you love; what do you love most. Love is Mary sitting at Jesus' feet, going to the source of love and listening to Him—quietly, undistracted, not rushing around the kitchen getting dinner ready. I like the idea of the one thing being love. I understand it, it makes sense; but I believe there is something else, something more specific, especially in light of this story. There must be something else that doesn't contradict love as the answer but complements it.

It just so happens that some scholars believe the "one thing" could mean one thing to eat or even a few things to eat.[8] Jesus could be saying, "We don't need everything you are making. We just need something you are making, so stop what you are doing, unplug for a while, sit down, relax and let's enjoy our time together."

Jesus didn't despise Martha for her behavior. He just corrected and encouraged her. In fact, He showed concern for her and implied His endearment of her when He said, "My dear Martha." I think that in our busy, daisy-chained moments of life, Jesus wants to speak lovingly to us as well, and I think Jesus would say something similar to what He said to Martha: "My dear parents, I know it's tough in this modern world of busyness and distraction. Believe it or not, I talked with others about this very issue when I was walking the earth hundreds of years ago. My words would apply today. There is only one thing worth being concerned about; stick to that. There is no need for more when only one will do."

It's Never Too Late to Start

If you are reading these words and saying, "I wish I had had this book three years ago (or seven years ago)," please don't look back with regret—look forward with hope. It's never too late to start anything. When you read the last three chapters of this book on writing a family purpose statement, family core values and priorities, you need to know that Mary and I didn't write ours 15 years ago, or 9 years ago. As I write this sentence, I want you to know that we wrote them 12 months ago, with teenage kids. My point? *You can start now.*

Many of us who have older children are still trying to play catch-up. We are just now identifying what the heck happened over the last few years! The modern family concept didn't slowly creep up on us over the last few years so that we had it figured out; it advanced rapidly and doesn't show signs of slowing down any time soon. So even if you're getting in the game late, take heed of the instructions in the book of Hebrews: "So take a new grip with your tired hands and strengthen your weak knees. Mark out a straight path for your feet so that those who are weak and lame will not fall but become strong" (Heb. 12:12-13).

I was doing a three-week series at a church that wanted me to come and talk about balanced living. After the last service of the first weekend, an elderly gentleman named Gary slowly made his way down the aisle toward the stage.

He told me he was 82 years old and then he thanked me for the message. He went on to tell me it was too late for him and his family. He told me he hadn't been the best parent and said he hadn't talked to his daughter in almost 40 years. I asked him why he thought it was too late. I could tell the wheels were spinning.

"Do you think it's too late for me to try to call her?"

"No! It's never too late!"

The following week after the last service, Gary again made his way toward the stage. "I called my daughter," he said without a smile. I asked what happened. He told me that the conversation hadn't gone as well as he had hoped it would. I asked him how he had expected the conversation to go.

After a few minutes of listening to him, I realized that Gary's expectation had been a bit too high. He assumed all would be back to normal after the first phone call. I said, "Gary, you haven't talked to your daughter in 40 years! Did you honestly think life would suddenly return to normal? What did happen?"

He told me he had had a short, civil conversation with his daughter and although the conversation hadn't been friendly, they had set up a time to talk again in the coming week.

"Gary, are you kidding me? That's a huge win." What I had really wanted to say was, "You should be happy that she took your call at all!" Baby steps, Gary, baby steps.

What matters is not how fast you move but the direction you move. So start now.

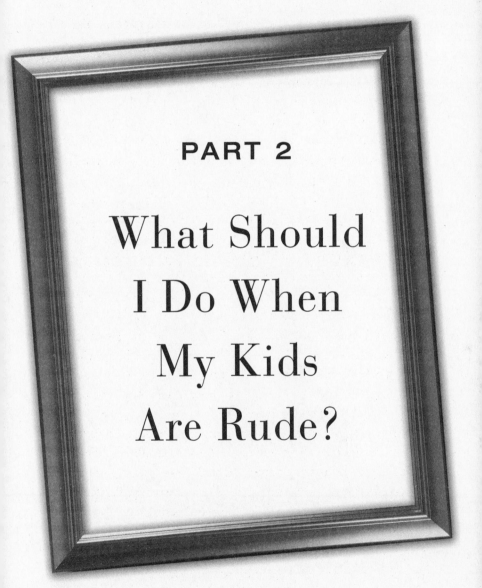

PART 2

What Should I Do When My Kids Are Rude?

4

Model the Behavior
You Want

Children have never been very good at listening to their parents,
but they have never failed to imitate them.
JAMES BALDWIN, AMERICAN AUTHOR

Rude behavior comes naturally. I know you didn't need me to tell you that, but I want you to note something. Think about your behavior during the past week. How did you do personally with your behavior? Were you constantly positive and encouraging with your words, voice and tone? How about your nonverbal communication cues? Were they positive, empowering and life giving? You may think back upon your past week and say, "Yes, there have been a few extremely rude people, but I have always returned that rude behavior with a kind look and an encouraging word." Okay, I applaud you. Well done! Keep it up. My behavior, on the other hand, has not been quite so positive.

Now that I am a little older, I have gained this remarkable ability to rationalize or justify my behavior to make myself look better, while I paint the other person as rude. I don't know if you have been given or have received this ability yet. It usually comes at the onset of adolescence and gets perfected over time.

It can be very easy to spot rude or unacceptable behavior in your friends' kids, but your own precious angels? Well, there may not be a disrespectful, rule-breaking bone in their bodies. Rudeness isn't just a child or adolescent trait. In fact, I see it more in adults than in children.

Not too long after Mary and I got married, we were quietly standing in line together at the grocery store. Suddenly, in the distance we could hear them coming—what sounded like a pack of wild animals fighting to the death. What actually appeared were a mom and her three kids, all under the age of seven, who were arguing over what cereal to buy.

A box was being passed between the two tallest children while the younger one screamed with hands stretched toward the heavens and feet rapidly pounding the floor.

Mom was pushing the basket leisurely around the corner while reading a food label on an item she had just taken from the shelf. She appeared unfazed by the volume and the antics. She calmly placed the item she was holding into her basket and got in line behind us. The tantrum over the cereal box had moved on to claim new territory: the gum and candy display that the horrible people at the grocery store had so conveniently placed alongside the checkout line. Now the loud dispute centered around the choice of gum and quickly escalated into a situation involving at least one headlock. Mom, again apparently not fazed by the uproar, casually thumbed through a magazine.

Mary and I were stunned. It was at that moment in our married-with-no-children brains that we thought, *Our children will never act that way!* And we continued to believe that pipedream for quite some time—all the way up until the time we had kids.

Fast-forward nine years. We stood in line at the grocery store with our twin four-year-old boys. They were arguing over a box of cereal, and Mary and I were arguing over gum. Out of the corner of my eye, I saw a recently married couple with no kids. (Yes, I could tell.) After observing our behavior, the guy turned as if to say something to his wife; before he could speak a word, I said, "Don't. Don't even say it." I knew what he was thinking. It was the same thing Mary and I had thought nine years ago. Lesson learned.

Rude Behavior

You could quickly and easily come up with a list of rude behaviors you've experienced, but I'll just give a short list I created in response to a quick question I posted on Facebook and Twitter.

- Being noisy in a public place
- Interrupting others while they are talking
- Not greeting others politely
- Using inappropriate language
- Putting others down
- Being disrespectful to parents
- Using a phone or other electronic device while talking with others
- Displaying an ungrateful attitude
- Talking loudly on a cellphone while sitting next to someone who's trying to write a book on the family while drinking a non-fat caramel macchiato at Starbucks (but I digress)

Once on a flight from Orange County, California, to Dallas, Texas, I had a middle seat near the rear of the plane. It really wasn't a bad seat, because there was nobody else sitting in the back of the plane. I had planned to do a little work and thought it would be great to have some room to spread out and not be distracted. God had other plans. The last people to board the plane that day were a mom and her two young children. I heard them before I saw them. "Mom, Mom, Mom, hey, Mom, MOM!" They walked down the aisle passing several open seats.

Having gone through previous situations of God working in my life, I should have known where the mom and kids were going to sit; but you can't blame a guy for trying, can you? Anyway, they ended up sitting right behind me. Everybody got buckled in and we were off. Of course there was constant verbal energy behind me, and in all honesty, I was okay with it. (Actually, I found myself waiting for them to say something I could write down to use as an illustration.) Unfortunately, after about 45 minutes, the children discovered the trays that drop down from the seat in front of you. Up, down, up, down, slam, smack, bang—times two. The mom surely knew what was happening. I mean this wasn't like the grocery store where the mom's attention could be captured by a lot of things. What could be so engrossing her mind that she was neglecting to parent her children?

Then, the banging of the trays stopped as suddenly as it had begun. *Wonderful*, I thought, but only for a moment. The reason being, the children had found a new activity—the one involving their legs and the seats in front of them. Although their legs weren't long enough to touch the floor, they *were* long enough to reach the seats in front of them. I'm not sure all kids like to slouch all the way down in their seats until the seatbelts ride up to their chins, but these kids did. Meanwhile their feet pushed against the seat in front of them to help them sit back up. And when that behavior was repeated 30, maybe 40 times, it became irritating.

Just when I could feel my blood begin to boil from this irritating behavior, it was time for sugar and peanuts from the flight attendants. The sugar was instant energy and the peanuts were ammunition. A coke was spilled, peanuts were thrown and mom kept saying, "You need to stop. You need to stop!" I had even made the courtesy turn-around-while-looking-through-the-space-between-the-seatbacks glare but received no acknowledgment from mom and only a mocking smile from one of the kids. His hand started moving toward me, making a pinching sign while he squinted one eye, and it was enough to scare me back to looking forward again.

The excessive activity coupled with the minor food fight and sheer volume of noise finally prompted one of the flight attendants to visit our area of the plane. You know kids are being rude when the flight attendant says to a parent, "Excuse me, would you mind if your kids played outside?" Actually, she didn't say that, although to my way of thinking it would have been a fair request. The flight attendant actually put the trays back up and told the kids they could not use the trays anymore, and she told the children that they needed to use their respectful hands and inside voices.

Except for providing me with a story that is only now amusing to tell, the flight got me to where I needed to go, and that's about it.

Things Are Caught, Not Taught

How we behave as parents will greatly affect how our kids behave. The words of the proverb are true: "The apple doesn't fall too far from the tree." The maxim reminds us that all children are similar to their parents, and it's not just in regard to appearance.

In Gilda Radner's book *It's Always Something*, she recounts a story from her childhood:

When I was little, [Dibby's] cousin had a dog, just a mutt, and the dog was pregnant. I don't know how long dogs are pregnant, but she was due to have her puppies in about a week. She was out in the yard one day and got in the way of the lawn mower, and her two hind legs got cut off. They rushed her to the vet and he said, "I can sew her up, or you can put her to sleep if you want, but the puppies are okay. She'll be able to deliver the puppies."

Dibby's cousin said, "Keep her alive."

So the vet sewed up her backside and over the next week the dog learned to walk. She didn't spend any time worrying, she just learned to walk by taking two steps in the front and flipping up her backside, and then taking two steps and flipping up her backside again. She gave birth to six little puppies, all in perfect health. She nursed them and then weaned them. And when they learned to walk, they all walked like her, taking two steps in the front and flipping up their backside.[1]

Why did the puppies walk like their mother? Because babies are great imitators of their parents. What this means is that we need to model the behavior for our children that we want to see in our children. Deuteronomy 6:5-6 gives us an understanding of what we should do and where we should start:

> And you must love the LORD your God with all your heart, all your soul, and all your strength. And you must commit yourselves wholeheartedly to these commands that I am giving you today.

A Good Example or a Terrible Warning

In one of her mysteries (*His Burial Too*), writer Catherine Aird wrote, "If you can't be a good example, then you'll just have to be a horrible warning."[2] I have been both. The good news is, if as a parent you have been a terrible warning at one time or another, you can choose to be a good example starting immediately. Parents do make mistakes and parents show rude behavior from time to time. But such behavior doesn't have to be part of your permanent make-up.

I'm sure as a parent you have looked in the mirror and thought, *That wasn't my best moment.* I have. Several years ago while on a family vacation, I had one such "not my best moment." We were driving around a busy town I didn't know very well. My driving ability has come under criticism from time to time while all of the family is in the vehicle. This was no exception.

I approached a green light in heavy traffic too quickly and passionately accelerated as it turned yellow and then slammed on the brakes when it turned red. I found myself partially in the intersection and completely in the crosswalk. There were several people using the crosswalk. Most of them walked around the front of the car with no feedback for me. A few looked to get a glimpse of the driver, and some glared. One pedestrian used a hand signal to signal his displeasure, but one used his foot—to kick the bumper.

The kick was loud enough for everyone to hear and hard enough to shake the car. I know what I should have done, because I did the opposite, and hindsight usually sees clearly. I rolled down the window to ask a question. Before I could get the words out of my mouth, the gentleman told me who I was and what he thought of me. I rolled up the window and pushed down common sense. When the light turned green, I pulled out into the intersection and should have kept going, but I didn't. I turned at the next light, and guess who was walking down the street? A divine appointment, right? I caught up to the gentleman and his wife and got out of the car. I walked over to the gentleman and had a very brief, very direct conversation and then got back into the car.

You can imagine the fun we had in the car as I drove away.

Apologize in Full

How do you explain that exceptional piece of parental modeling to your spouse, to your kids? "Go and do likewise" won't get it done. "Do as I say, not as I do" is dumb advice. "Sorry about that" doesn't get it done either. It's hard to swallow your pride as a parent; at least that's been my experience. We teach our children that when they apologize, they need to say it all. "Sorry" doesn't work. "Sorry about that" doesn't work. In our home, we require three things of an apology.

1. *You must own your behavior with that first word: "I." "*I am sorry for . . ."
2. *You verbalize what you did wrong.* ". . . getting out of the car and yelling at those people. I made a poor choice with my actions . . ."
3. *You ask forgiveness of those you have offended.* "Will you please forgive me?"

There is a great verse in the book of Romans: "And do your best to live at peace with everyone" (Rom. 12:18, *CEV*). Notice that the verse doesn't say, "Kids, do your best to live at peace with everyone." Nor does it say, "Parents, do your best to live at peace with everyone." The instruction is for all of us to do our best—parents and children alike.

I like what Ephesians 6:4 says in *THE MESSAGE*: "Fathers, don't exasperate your children by coming down hard on them. Take them by the hand and lead them in the way of the Master." That's it, isn't it? We are to demonstrate a gentle spirit and admit when we have blown it. Leading your children in the way of the Master is a far cry from digging your heels in and trying to justify your unjustifiable behavior of, let's say, trying to find a guy who kicked the bumper of your car so you could talk some sense into him. However, sitting down in a quiet moment and asking their forgiveness is.

Lead by a Skillful Hand

With an example of a certain parent's poor choice fresh on your mind, I think we should take a look at our theme verse for this book: "He cared for them with a true heart and led them with skillful hands" (Ps. 78:72). This reference to how David was to lead Israel as he had led his father's flock of sheep paints a wonderful picture for me as a parent. It is a reminder for each of us as parents to have a soft, true and gentle heart, not a heart of pushiness, frustration or exasperation. We are reminded here that it is equally important to lead with skill.

The words "led them with skillful hands" cause me to think about two different and unique pictures in my mind when it comes to parenting my kids. The first picture is one of frustration. There is a battle of the wills taking place. Imagine, if you will, a scene in which I have asked my son Alec several times to put down the toy he has and come to me. He does not move; he does not budge at all. I am now engaged in a staring match with my son.

- "Alec, please put that toy down and come here."
- "No."
- "Alec, this is the last time I am going to tell you to put down that toy and get over here, now."
- "No, no, no. Mine!"

So I move toward him while he begins the loud audio portion of the encounter, and I pry the toy from his hand, place it on the ground, *grab him by the wrist* and move him to where I want him to be.

The second picture is one of patience. This, too, involves a battle of the wills. I have asked my son Alec several times to put down the toy and come here. He does not budge. I am now in a staring match with my son.

- "Alec, please put that toy down and come here."
- "No."
- "Alec, this is the last time I am going to tell you to put down that toy and get over here, now."
- "No, no, no. Mine!"

So I move toward him while he begins the loud audio portion of the encounter and I pry the toy from his hand, place it on the ground, take him *by the hand* and lead him to where I want him to be.

The only difference in these two pictures is how we lead. One picture is usually reactionary while the other tends to be revolutionary. Are you leading by taking the wrist or by holding the hand?

Teaching Healthy Values

I hope you can see by now that, as parents, we are teaching even if we have no agenda. We are teaching when we are rude or respectful, when we are angry or compassionate, when we are walking or when we are talking. We are teaching all the time. The more time we are with our kids, the clearer our message becomes. In order to teach our children healthy values, we must absorb them first and model them to our children. Since most people like lists, me included, I will give you a list. But this is not a list of values to teach your children. No, the following list is for you and me to practice as parents:

1. Humility
2. Respect
3. Kindness
4. Honesty
5. Courage
6. Perseverance
7. Self-discipline
8. Compassion
9. Generosity
10. Dependability

Now, that's a good list, isn't it? Google "parents' values" or ask other parents on Facebook and you will get a similar list. A list isn't the hard part; practicing the list is the hard part. Printing the list and hanging it on the refrigerator is a great idea. We have done similar things as parents. When a list is visible, it can serve as a reminder and help prompt you to make better, wiser choices, and I understand that. But simply memorizing a list, even the 10 Commandments, has little to no value when stored in your short-term memory. "Most of the information kept in short-term memory will be stored for approximately 20 to 30 seconds,"[3] which is hardly enough time to bring about life change. Short-term memory does not affect long-term behavior. What does affect long-term behavior is consistent performance over time, or modeling. It's unfair to expect our kids to listen to what we say and ignore our example.

My advice to you is, don't worry about teaching lists to your kids. Practice the list as a parent. Your example will teach your kids the qualities on the list. Experts have a word for this kind of modeling and absorbing of behavior: "incidental learning, a process by which children identify with and imitate their parents."[4]

As we go about our day, we need to remind ourselves that we go as teachers, especially around our children. Just like a sponge, they absorb what we intentionally pour and accidentally spill. I prefer the intentional reminder, so here are five areas worth modeling to your children.

1. Manage Your Time

How we manage time as parents will be absorbed by our kids. Involve your older kids in the discussion about whom you will spend your time with and where that time will be spent. Discuss the importance of not overdoing anything and trying to have balance. Remind them it's okay to sit quietly and read or sit quietly and create or meditate. Meditating on God's Word has become a lost art in our modern world. "Don't act thoughtlessly, but understand what the Lord wants you to do" (Eph. 5:17).

2. Open Your Heart

Having a big heart toward others is a valuable behavior for our children to see modeled because it shows love, kindness, honor, value and respect for others. Opening a door for someone as you enter a building, helping someone in your neighborhood, going on a mission trip to serve the poor—there are many things that can be done to show that you have a big heart. "By everything I did, I showed how you should work to help everyone who is weak. Remember that our Lord Jesus said, 'More blessings come from giving than from receiving'" (Acts 20:35, *CEV*).

3. Date Your Family

The family that plays together stays together. Having fun and laughing together help to form a bond between everyone and teaches the entire family not to take life too seriously. Laughing together is the glue that holds people together. On a scientific level "laughing represents the shortest distance between people because it instantly interlocks the limbic systems of the brain. It's no surprise, then, that people who enjoy each other's company laugh easily and often."[5] Even the Bible subscribes to the good that laughing can do:

I recommend having fun, because there is nothing better for people to do in this world than to eat, drink, and enjoy life. That way they will experience some happiness along with all the hard work God gives them (Eccles. 8:15).

4. Encourage Your Family

There are so many ways to live a life that encourages others—the words we say, the looks we give, the gifts we share. Maintaining a positive attitude in situations that are difficult is also encouraging. Speaking into the life of each of your kids with a positive tone and life-giving words is encouraging. Writing a note to your spouse and/or each of your children and leaving it in a place where they will easily find it encourages them. Bringing home a "Friday surprise" for everyone in your family lifts their spirits. As parents we want to "keep on encouraging each other to be thoughtful and to do helpful things" (Heb. 10:24, CEV).

5. Learn from Difficulty

I honestly wish we could avoid this one altogether, but finding joy even in difficult times is a necessary area and an important skill to pass on to our children. James 1:2-3 says, "Dear brothers and sisters, when troubles come your way, consider it an opportunity for great joy. For you know that when your faith is tested, your endurance has a chance to grow." James says "when," not "if," trouble comes our way. And when trouble comes our way, we are given powerful moments for modeling the right behavior. Some characteristics are forged only in pain, brokenness and difficulty—characteristics like tenacity, resilience, humility, thankfulness, leadership, trust and faith. Scripture reminds us that God's "kindness is all you need. My power is strongest when you are weak." Paul went on to say, "So if Christ keeps giving me his power, I will gladly brag about how weak I am" (2 Cor. 12:9, CEV). Now that's something to boast about in front of your children!

I believe the toughest part of parenting is the constant modeling of behavior without a break or momentary reprieve. We simply can't model the right behavior all the time. So, we do the best we can. We listen, learn, watch, read, think and talk about how to be better as parents—not perfect parents, just better parents by making an effort to learn what we can so that we will model the best we can, every opportunity we can.

Your Family Rhythm

What I like best about families is that each member is different. We look different, we act differently and we're interested in different things. Each member has his or her own rhythm and beat. In a musical sense, rhythm is "The pattern of musical movement through time."[6] I'm sure you have heard someone described as "marching to the beat of his [or her] own drum." Usually that means the person has an internal beat or rhythm that is different from most people. It's a statement about uniqueness and style.

We have many different instruments in our families. In fact, if you have a bigger family, you have a bigger band! But no matter how many people are in your band, the goal is to always keep the rhythm! Why march to the beat of the music playing across the street in someone else's family when you have everything you need to create your own family rhythm? What I am talking about here is being in sync and resonant with each other. It's how you keep in step and are melodic and harmonious within your family. And each family must find its own rhythm, the beat that makes that family unique.

What interests and activities are unique to your family? Do you like to camp? Do you like to rough it out in nature? Do you like to rough it at the Marriott downtown? Me too. One way is neither right nor wrong. But the interests your family pursues together *are* important. In order to maintain rhythm in your family, you need to have something that is consistent, a musical beat that everyone can follow.

Once you've established the rhythm, the key to making music rather than noise is to make sure everyone in your family is playing the same song. When everyone is together, your family resounds with music and rhythm! You can feel it and others can see it.

One of the interesting observations we have made as parents is that sometimes our kids want to write or play for the band down the street. We have been told they have "better management" and get to do things the kids in our band don't get to do. They get to "play different venues" or "better locations" and have a better "contract" than the kids playing in our band. I'm sure you have heard some of these same stories from your own band members. It's okay. Just keep teaching the instruments you have in your home and keep the beat and rhythm going. All the musicians in your band will eventually get on board. You may sing off-key for a while, but you will find the right key in no time.

When your family is singing off-key it's easy to hear. The sound is dissonant, nothing flows and there is unrelieved tension in the air. The bottom line is . . . it's not good. When you are off-key, you have moved from resonance to dissonance. "Dissonance" is a term we can apply to our musical thoughts. If you have ever attended a concert and heard the band playing and singing in harmony, but one member of the band misses a chord, or a singer sings the wrong note, that's dissonance. Think of that scrunched-up facial expression of pain you make when you are listening to a beautiful song and hear a wrong note. That's dissonance, and dissonance sounds the same in the band as it does in the family; it requires those who are "not playing along" or keeping the beat to make an adjustment.

Emotionally dissonant families tend to be off-key. It could be from a lack of conducting from the bandleader or even a misunderstanding of what music or instrument everyone is playing. But when your family is in sync and has found its internal rhythm, you can feel it and you can see it and you can sense it. Everybody is on the same note at the same time. Sure, everyone misses a note occasionally. When that happens, you can point fingers and blame or you can give a hug and encouragement. The simple fact is that each member of your family, each member of your band, is unique, with a different personality and with different skills and abilities. That's where style comes in. What kind of band are you? Here are five suggestions.

1. **Rock 'n' Roll**

   Some families are rock 'n' roll! Simple words, straight-forward melodies, energetic beat and having fun! I'm partial to 80s rock simply because it was and still is the best. I love when my kids hear one of the classic songs from the 80s on their favorite Spotify or XM Radio channel, and Mary or I start singing along. Karimy will say, "How do you know that song? That's one of our songs." No, sweetie, that's a copy of the original and, yes, it did sound better in 1988. Is your family passionate, full of energy and occasionally loud? Then maybe your family style is a rock 'n' roll band.

2. **Classical**

   Some families may take a more serious, conventional approach to life. Classical families are usually tradition oriented, quiet and make a point of following plans that have been well thought out in advance. Classical music lovers may be a bit more conservative and probably have long family traditions. There's passion, but the approach is clearer and more easily followed. How about your family? Does your family's band style share a classical component?

3. **Jazz**

   Jazz is musical art. A jazz family band sees things differently. They're the Picassos of musical play. On occasion, everyone in the family band may appear not to be playing the same song, but the creatively trained ear can pick up an underlying rhythm that keeps everyone together while creating individuality. Jazz makes sense to those who are open to spontaneity but may not resonate with anyone else. If your family is artsy and expressive, creative and spontaneous, you may have a jazz family band.

4. **Pop**

   A pop family band is interested in things that are culturally relevant and that have lots of generational appeal. Members of a pop band display a lot of harmony and a dance party vibe! Fun, entertaining and energetic, a pop family band isn't the life of the party—they *are* the party! Is your family outgoing, energetic and fun? Your family's style could be pop!

5. **Country**

   Players in a country band seek authentic experiences that are informal and uncomplicated. They are generally laid-back and transparent and down to earth. Though passionate about life and how to live it, country players are very casual and enjoy the simple things in life. Is your family pretty relaxed and relationally connected? You may have a little country band going in your family.

Although I've spent some time describing five of the types of music your family band may play, the genre isn't as important as the rhythm. Find your rhythm and then define your style. The two most important things to remember as a family are (1) stay in sync as a family, and (2) find your unique style.

I opened this chapter with a story about how Mary and I once thought that our kids would never act "that way." Well, as you know, they did and they have. What's worse is that I have acted "like that" as an adult! Maybe not throwing a tantrum over a piece of candy, like a four-year-old at the register of a grocery store, but I have thrown a four-year-old-like tantrum in a restaurant because the service was poor. Which is worse, a four-year-old-like tantrum in a four-year-old body, or a four-year-old-like tantrum in a forty-year-old body? The first is expected (or at least, not unexpected); the second is unfortunate.

Just remember when that four-year-old child begins to surface in your adult body and manages to wiggle its way out into public view, there's still a chance. There's still a chance to model the right behavior through humility, authenticity and forgiveness. How amazing is that!

5

Repeat the Behavior
You Want

There is no harm in repeating a good thing.
PLATO, GREEK PHILOSOPHER

As a parent, do you ever feel like you are repeating yourself? "I think that my son needs to be disciplined more. I'm sick of having to repeat myself to my son when I tell him to do something that he doesn't want to do." "I have to repeat myself all the time. Put the cats down, no jumping on the bed, no standing on the couch, no running in the house. It gets on my nerves. I have to say it every five minutes or so." "I repeat myself so much I feel like a broken record." (What's a record?)

Repeating ourselves is part of a parent's job description. We are reminded in Deuteronomy 6:7: "Repeat them [the commands] again and again to your children. Talk about them when you are at home and when you are on the road, when you are going to bed and when you are getting up." Before we talk about what to repeat, let's talk about the word "repeat."

When I see or hear the word "repeat" within the context of parenting, I get exhausted. "Can you please turn off the light? Turn off the light, turn it off, turn it off, turn it off! Can you please take out the trash? Take out the trash, take it out, take it out, take it out! Can you please turn off the game? Turn off the game, turn it off, turn it off, turn it off! Can you please pick up your clothes, pick up your clothes, pick them up, pick them up, pick them up!"

The word "repeat" in Deuteronomy 6:7 is translated from a Hebrew word that actually means "whet."[1] Now, I don't know about you, but I rarely use the word "whet"; in fact, let me take that back and say I never use the word "whet." The best way to understand this word in a modern way is to think about how to sharpen a knife. I don't know how you sharpen a knife at your house, but in our house we plug in a knife sharpener and run the blade through it a few times and we're done. That was not the case when Deuteronomy was written. If you wanted to sharpen your knife while you were walking around with Moses, you needed both your knife and a stone, specifically a whetstone. You would sharpen the blade of your knife by running it over the whetstone at the correct angle with consistent, even pressure and keep repeating that movement until your knife was sharp.

If you have ever sharpened a knife using a whetstone, you know it takes time, skill, patience and understanding. Ironically, you could say the same thing about parenting! When the writer of Deuteronomy penned the words "repeat them again and again to your children," he was giving us a picture not only of what parenting is like but also of what we need to do. What should we do when our kids are rude? We start by modeling the behavior we want and then we keep repeating the behavior and talking about the behavior over and over and over again.

How to Be a Sharp Parent

1. Time

When you use a whetstone to sharpen a knife, you must run the blade over the whetstone more than once. It would be great if we could make one pass over the stone and be done. Unfortunately, that isn't the case. It would also be great if we could tell our children one time to be truthful and have it happen. Or tell them one time to pick up their room or turn out the lights or take out the trash, but that hasn't been our experience with our kids. What sharpens a knife is consistent, even pressure over time. I hope you caught those two words "consistent" and "even." In other words, you want to be unchanging and steady (or level), not going to one extreme or another. The two most common extremes are peerenting and powerenting. Most of the parenting books encourage us to avoid such extremes, and I agree.

Someone who is peerenting is trying to act like his or her child's best friend.[2] It's hard to parent when you want to be your child's best friend. You can certainly help each of your children see what makes a good friend and what characteristics to look for in a friend, and you can teach and model the healthy behavior of a good friend. However, peerenting is usually just an attempt to be a cool parent, to be "in" and relevant with your child.

There came a point in the lives of my kids when I went from cool to a fool. Although neither Mary nor I have ever tried to peerent our children, I have told my kids several times that we (Mary and I) are cool. After all, I knew that other kids think we are cool. It's just our kids who don't think we are cool. I have asked them, "Who do you think are cool parents?" Each one has rattled off a few names, and I think to myself, *Are you serious? Those parents aren't cool. We are cool!* At least I only went from cool to fool in my mind, not out loud.

Here's the general law of being a cool parent: Your children will think every parent except you is cool. And that's it. As Phil Dunphy, the dad in the *Modern Family* television show, would say about parenting, "Act like a parent, talk like a peer. I call it peerenting."[3] I, however, would say, "Act like a parent, talk like a parent, because you are the parent." Parenting isn't a popularity contest; it's a responsibility we must take seriously.

The opposite of peerenting is powerenting. Because parents are bigger and stronger than their children, they may want to exercise control of their children through strength and power, and not have any sort of relationship at all with their children. Generally speaking, rules without relationship will lead to rebellion, especially as kids get older. Powerenting—the "my way or the highway" style of parenting—causes children to shut down emotionally and relationally over time. An authoritarian parent is not responsive to his or her child's needs and sees everything in black and white. Powerenting is about rules and rigidity, enforcement and punishment to keep kids in line. Just as with peerenting, powerenting will do more damage than good.

2. Skill

Using a whetstone to sharpen a knife requires skill. Skill is usually achieved over time with lots of practice and experience. We have neither when we are first blessed with children. So how do we learn to be better parents? By reading what God's Word has to say, by reading parenting books written by experts in the field, by talking to other parents, and by having open and honest communication with our kids.

Skill to sharpen the blade of a knife on a whetstone also includes maintaining the same angle as you run the blade across the stone, sharpening both sides of the blade evenly. Similarly, maintaining the same angle and approach in our parenting is also necessary; in other words, both parents must be on the same page. After you run one side of the blade down the stone a few times, you must turn the blade over and run that side at the same angle to sharpen the knife evenly. The thought here for us as parents is to be on the same page.

If each parent has a different parenting philosophy, maintaining the same "sharpening angle" with your children will be tough, if not impossible. Whether you are just thinking about having kids, or you already have kids, talk with your spouse about the importance of having the same approach to parenting. If the two of you are not on the same parenting page, or you feel like your spouse isn't even reading the same book, skip ahead to part 4 of this book where I talk about the importance of having a stable foundation, family vision and mission statement, values and goals. Those things will really bring alignment to your family as you move forward together.

3. Patience

If you pray for patience as a couple, you will probably end up with strong-willed children. I stopped praying for patience after our third child, and we haven't had any children since. Of course, that's a mild attempt at humor, but there also is a grain of truth to that statement. Kids will test the patience of their parents to the point of absolute exhaustion. So, before going any further, let's all take a deep breath and read Galatians 6:9 out loud: "Let's not get tired of doing what is good. At just the right time we will reap a harvest of blessing if we don't give up." You may want to highlight that verse or write it out on a card to carry with you or spray paint it on the mirror just to remind you to patiently hang in there!

Now, there are some kids who are just easy. Their personalities and demeanors are such that they listen to everything you say, do everything you ask them to do. Life is great—a regular bowl of cherries. We have some friends who will say, "Our daughter is just easy." That's the word they use: "easy." Well, if your children are like that, then good for you. Fantastic. I am so excited for you. (Was my sarcasm too subtle?) Just know that you are blessed, and move on. For the parents who are blessed with strong-willed, defiant children who must touch the stove to see if it's hot, let me tell you a story.

We have a friend who has a strong-willed child named Tyler. To be fair, strong-willed is an understatement. We were getting together one morning and Karen, Tyler's mom, was late. We started to worry a bit since Karen was rarely, if ever, late to anything. We were sitting in front of Starbucks when she pulled up in her car. *Great,* we thought, *everything is okay.* When she got out of her car, we could tell she wasn't okay; in fact, she looked frazzled. She stumbled over to us and sat down. "What's wrong?" we asked her. She went on to tell us about the experience she had just had with her son that morning.

Karen told us she had needed to pick up a few things for Tyler to take to school before dropping him off there. Before going into the store, she had told Tyler they didn't have a lot of time and they would only be able to walk in, get what they needed and walk out. That's it. Well, apparently Tyler wanted to stop by the toy aisle, but his mom explained to him they would only have time to get what they needed and then leave. So, when they got out of the car, Tyler asked again about stopping by the toy aisle. Karen told him no. Right there in the parking lot, Tyler took a deep breath and held it. He held it until he passed out! After reviving Tyler, Karen took him by the hand and they went into the store to get what they needed. Despite every attempt to navigate around the toy aisle, they found themselves standing across from it. Tyler made the move toward the aisle and his mom repeated herself, letting him know they did not have time to stop and look at the toys. Once again, Tyler took a deep breath and . . . you guessed it: he held it until he passed out again! *Strong will?*

I'm sure you are as curious as we were about Tyler's unique behavior. When I heard that story, the questions ran through my mind. *How often did this happen? Frequently? What do you do when he passes out? Do you put him in a cart and push him around? Do you grab him by the hand and drag him across the floor? Is that illegal? What do other parents say? How long does it take for him to wake up?* The only question I spoke out loud was, "What happened next?"

There was no verbal response for several moments as Karen leaned over into her large purse and started rummaging around. I wasn't sure what she was doing or what she was looking for. To my surprise, she pulled out a squirt bottle half full of water and set it on the table. We stared at the bottle. *Why the bottle?* I wondered. Karen turned to me and said, "When he holds his breath and passes out, I reach into my bag and pull out that bottle." It must have been obvious to Karen that I was not tracking the point of the bottle and why it was half empty. So she added, "Then I squirt him a few times until he wakes up." *What? Are you serious?* I wanted to ask if the bottle started out full that morning, but it felt rude and disrespectful, so I kept my mouth shut. I tried to think of a Bible verse that could "speak" to that kind of parenting moment, but the best I could come up with was "Thou shalt not squirt thy child" (Hallucinations 3:7). (Sorry, but I couldn't resist writing that, because I definitely thought it.)

I really wish there was a specific verse for every specific parenting moment, but there isn't. However, there are many verses that remind us, encourage us and equip us as parents. One such verse is, "Don't be quick to get angry, because anger is typical of fools. Don't ask, 'Why were things better in the old days than they are now?' It isn't wisdom that leads you to ask this" (Eccles. 7:9-10, *GOD'S WORD*).

If we are diligent at learning parenting skills and applying patience to what we have learned and are still learning, then we are where we should be.

4. Understanding

At some point, every parent faces the "That's not fair!" conversation. Those words and "Why do they get to and I don't?" are probably the two most repeated phrases in a home with children.

> Child: "Why do I have to be 14 to have a Facebook account? Facebook says I can have one when I am 13!"
> Parent: "I know Facebook says you can have an account when you're 13, but as your parent, I say you need to be 14."
> Child: "That's not fair."
> Parent: "Life isn't fair."

Have you had that conversation? It may not have been about a social media site, but no matter what the subject, the course of the conversation was probably similar. Frustrating to parents? Yes! Necessary conversation? Yes! Will you have to repeat this conversation? Yes! Sharpening a knife requires understanding how many times you will need to sharpen one side of the knife blade before turning it over and sharpening the other side. How many times will you be able to use your knife before having to sharpen it again? How often will my kids tell me their lives are unfair? Being aware and mindful of our children's needs and how they are feeling is an important part of parenting.

"Go to your room!" Have you ever uttered those words? Understanding your child's personality and needs will define whether or not those words are a consequence or reward. When our children were younger, two of them didn't like the consequence of their free time being taken away from them. They did not like being sent to their respective room, so that was definitely a punishment. However, one of our children loved being in his room! That was an opportunity to sit and read a book. Being sent to his room was like winning an award to him. If you were to say to him, "Today is your day, and we are going to reward you with anything you want. How about a day at Disneyland, or some ice cream?" He would say, "I would like to sit in my room and read a book." Understanding our children's gifts, abilities, talents and personalities is important for us to know as parents, because knowing these things helps us to make better decisions when correcting inappropriate behavior or reinforcing good behavior.

Five Family Routines Worth Repeating

You might feel as if repeating right and healthy behavior shouldn't continue ad nauseam, but to repeat what I have already said, repeating is part of a parent's job description. (Would you like me to repeat that?) One of the ways to make the repetition a bit easier is through the establishment of family routines. Routines are those planned, recurring activities and habits that add health and value to your family on a regular basis. What follows is a list of five simple routine ideas to try with your family. Find the one that works best for you or start with number one and work your way down to see which routine fits your family best.

1. Playing Together

The family that plays together stays together! We like having fun as a family. Most everything we do turns into a game. I don't know if it's everyone's competitive nature in our family or that we just like to play; either way, we find ourselves playing. You don't necessarily have to play board games. I know that board games are spelled "bored" games for some families. What I am suggesting is that you get together—inside your home or outside—and have fun together. We all went on a hike recently, and while on the hike, we must have played eight different games. The "running ahead to see who could be first" game, the "hide and let's scare Mom and Dad" game, the "hide and let's scare Karimy game," the "you had better not scare her again or you will be grounded until Jesus comes back" game, and more. Playing together allows for spontaneous connections; and any routine that will put our families in a position for that to happen is worth repeating.

2. Reading Together

Reading together is an activity that can become a routine before your kids are born! We did. When Mary was pregnant with Alec and Cameron, we would read to her tummy several times a week; and right after they were born, we continued to read to them. The great news about this routine is that our kids have become avid readers to the point of sneaking a flashlight to bed when they were younger so they could stay up and finish a book past their bedtime. The downside is that our Kindle accounts are linked to the same credit card—mine. Let's just say I have made a significant investment in their reading hobby.

3. Eating Together

The more times per week you can have dinner together, the better. Researchers have found that the benefits for families who eat together vary "based on the frequency of weekly family meal times (i.e., low=0-2, medium=3-4, and high=5-7 meals)," and they have discovered "that medium and high levels (i.e., 3 or more days a week) of frequent meals yield the most positive benefits for children."[4]

Although more recent research about the benefits of eating dinner together as a family indicated that the benefits may not be as great as earlier thought, the studies did suggest a positive bottom line:

> Our findings suggest that the effects of family dinners on children depend on the extent to which parents use the time to engage with their children and learn about their day-to-day lives. So if you aren't able to make the family meal happen on a regular basis, don't beat yourself up: just find another way to connect with your kids.[5]

The president of the National Center for Addiction and Substance Abuse at Columbia University echoes the article by saying, "One of the simplest and most effective ways for parents to be engaged in their teens' lives is by having frequent family dinners."[6]

Eating dinner together, then, is a healthy routine worth instituting, but it's not necessarily an easy one. If you have not really put this into practice until now, you may say, "Piece of cake! How hard can it be to have dinner together?" I guess it depends on the dynamics of your family. When we made the switch in our family to dinner together four nights a week, we thought it would be a "piece o' cake" as well. However, we found out within the first few minutes of sitting down at the table that this would be something we would have to grow into.

The first questions we heard were "Why are we doing this?" "This is weird!" "Why do we have to eat together?" "Mumble, mumble, what, what?" And that was Mary and me! Just kidding. But our children did have an opinion, and the first two nights didn't go as planned, mostly because we didn't have a plan. We thought we would somehow mysteriously bond and connect over the carrots and peas, but we didn't. So, the following week, we started to play a game Mary put together from a list of questions and comments, and we called it "The Dinner Game"! Things got better from that point on.

Because I know what it's like to be unprepared walking into the "dinner zone," below are the 31 (one for each day of the month!)

open-ended statements we used to start connecting with our kids
as we ate together. If you are having a difficult time getting the
conversation going at dinner, use the conversation starters here
to get the ball rolling.

1. My family is unique because . . .
2. A question I'd like to ask my dad is . . .
3. My most valuable possession is . . .
4. I'm a great friend because . . .
5. My parents are proud of me because . . .
6. The funniest thing I ever did was . . .
7. The best thing about my dad is . . .
8. The best thing about my mom is . . .
9. The best thing about me is . . .
10. If dreams come true, I'd dream . . .
11. I'd like to tell my family that . . .
12. If my family could repeat a vacation, it would be . . .
13. I'm a great sister or brother because . . .
14. If I could redecorate my bedroom, I would . . .
15. I like to surprise my brother and sister by . . .
16. The best thing that happened to me this week was . . .
17. The best advice I've ever received was . . .
18. The best book I ever read is . . .
19. My favorite teacher is . . .
20. I would like to take my family to see . . .
21. The last time my family laughed together was . . .
22. When I grow up, I want to . . .
23. Today, God used me to . . .
24. My favorite Bible verse is . . .
25. One thing my grandparents say is . . .
26. The last time I told someone "I love you" was . . .
27. If I could give my family one thing, it would be . . .
28. If I could create a new family tradition, it would be . . .
29. The talent God blessed me with is . . .

30. My favorite holiday is . . .
31. The last person I gave a hug to was . . .

4. Mom and Dad Together

Since this is a book about the entire family, I feel it's important to talk about mom and dad time together as a routine, as well as family time as a routine. I certainly understand the season of married with three kids. I have talked about how being parents makes great demands on our time, and we have to be careful not to become over-committed; but what I have not yet mentioned is that as the family flame begins to spread, the spark of romance can die out. Spending time with your spouse, without your children, will make you a healthier parent. That's not just my experience and observation.

Michelle Weiner-Davis, author of a book titled *Divorce Busting*, wrote,

> I'm convinced that the single biggest contributor to the breakdown in relationships today is the fact that couples aren't spending enough time together. They aren't making their relationships a number one priority. The relationship gets put on the back burner. Everything else seems more important—careers, children, hobbies, community involvement, and personal pursuits. And when relationships aren't attended to as they should be, trouble sets in.[7]

That's a great point for each of us to repeat to ourselves as parents. Let's not forget to spend time together with our spouses.

But what if you are a single parent?

If your current season is single with kids, then I would suggest finding time when you can be with close friends. Being a single parent is difficult; trying to fill two roles is hard. While I have not been a single parent, I did grow up in a single-parent home, and I understand the importance of connecting with other like-minded adults and having close relationships with others.

5. Praying Together

Praying together as a family is another one of those routines that isn't easy to establish. Getting everyone together at the same time may seem like an impossible task, and let's not forget that most people don't like to pray out loud. In our family, I believe it's the last one that gets us stuck; but for most families the hardest thing to do is gathering everyone together.

One of the ways our family has solved the gathering problem is to pray together when we're in the car (eyes open!)—on the way to school, on the way to the grocery store—anytime at all is good, and now that our boys have started driving, we pray all the time in the car!

How about praying at dinnertime or at any meal you have together as a family? What about bedtime? Getting the whole family together just before going to bed is a great time to pray. You don't have to spend 30 minutes praying; how about three minutes? Ask God to go before you the next day and help all of you trust and rely on Him. You can also pray for your kids' friends, for protection for your family, for their activities and for any tests or quizzes they may have the next day. You can pray for their future spouse, for their career and for opportunities to serve others. You can pray for character traits, attitudes and relationships. The prayer list is endless.

Developing a prayer routine with your family encourages honesty and humility among each person in your family. When your teenager asks God for help in controlling his or her tongue and to help them watch what they say at school, or when they pray to be a better friend to someone, or they pray for a good friend they can hang out with, it is powerful. It opens up communication not just with God, but also among your family. Before you pray together the next day, you can ask, "How did God answer your prayer today about being a better friend to someone?" Praying together will draw your family closer and take your family deeper—guaranteed. And, as an added benefit, Jesus is right there with you. His Word reminds us, "Whenever two or three of you come together in my name, I am there with you" (Matt. 18:20, *CEV*). Yes, He is right there with you, guiding you, leading you, encouraging you and answering you. There is tremendous power in a prayer routine!

Don't Whet the Small Stuff

There are some things that happen in our homes that we need to strongly discourage, and there are some things we need to let go. We need to understand the difference between rude behavior and an innocent mistake. We need to see the difference between childish irresponsibility and direct defiance. Sometimes it's hard to know the difference and harder to respond as a parent. Let me give you an example.

Not long ago, our family was on vacation in Seattle. When you are in Seattle, and you are a Starbucks fan, you must visit the epicenter of all things Starbucks by paying your respects at the very first Starbucks location, in Pike Place Market. On this particular trip, our boys were in junior high, and they had a newfound love for the grande double chocolate chip Frappuccino with whipped cream and chocolate sauce.

Visiting Pike Place Market is an experience in itself; there are crowds of people, a bustle of activity, street performers, traffic, a dizzying array of booths, people buying and selling everything from flowers to fish. When we arrived at Starbucks, there were about 30 people in line and frenetic activity both inside and outside the store.

While we waited in line—getting bumped and jostled—I started to get irritated. I was especially getting annoyed with my boys. Squirrely, jumpy, fidgety and childish would be accurate, and that was describing me! Alec and Cameron were even worse. Usually when my irritation reaches its peak, it feels like it's about to erupt onto those around me. And I felt it coming on.

In the midst of all of this energy and activity, I noticed a seemingly out-of-place man sitting on the shelf in the corner of this very small Starbucks. Smelly and dirty, he appeared to be homeless; but he wasn't doing anything wrong. He was just sitting there. He was collecting stares from several other people besides me—all of us, I imagine, probably thinking the same thing: *He shouldn't be in the store.* I wasn't worried for the safety of my kids, but I did quietly tell them not to go near the man. We finally got to the head of the line and ordered our drinks; when they were ready, we headed for the door.

As we got near the man sitting on the shelf, I noticed my son Cameron off to the side, with his wallet open and crumpled bills falling out in front of him onto the floor. Although I didn't vocalize it, my first thought was, *Come on. Why are you digging through your wallet in the middle of this crowd and right in front of the door no less.* I prompted him to come outside. I preferred to lecture him on the street where others wouldn't see me as a bad parent. Cameron came strolling out with a few crumpled dollars in his right hand and the Frappuccino in his left.

In a sarcastic and irritated tone of voice, I said, "Did you want to buy something in there, because if you did, you should have done it earlier. You should have been prepared. And didn't I tell you not to go near that homeless guy? Why don't you listen?" Cameron replied that he didn't want to buy anything. "Then why on earth was your money out? You have to do a better job at keeping track of your money."

Cameron said, "Dad, I saw that homeless guy sitting there and no one was helping him, so I gave him some money. That's what we are supposed to do, right? We're supposed to help others."

Have you ever felt humility, pride, anger, compassion, joy and sadness all at the same time? That's what I felt in that moment. We have tried to raise our kids to have compassion for others—to extend grace and mercy to those in need and to help the poor and less fortunate. We want them to reach out and make a difference, and here I was giving a lecture to my son about paying attention and moving a little faster when the thing that slowed him down was his empathy for a homeless man—a man whom I had viewed as out of place and shouldn't be there.

So I have to ask, which dad is my son supposed to obey? The dad who has been trying to teach and model compassion and empathy, or the dad who told him to not go near the homeless man? Cameron had been directly defiant, because he had done what I told him *not* to do—go near the guy. But should there have been a consequence—a punishment—for this disobedient choice?

I will tell you, one parent to another, no consequence (punishment) was called for; and if anything needed to be done, I should have been put in a time-out. Parents aren't perfect and we aren't raising robots (nor do we want to). As our children get older, we want them to take the values we have tried to instill in them and practice them independently from us; and that's exactly what Cameron was doing. "Young people don't always do what they're told, but if they can pull it off and do something wonderful, sometimes they escape punishment."[8] And I would add, *should* escape the punishment.

The same is true for getting mad at your five-year-old for spilling his or her third glass of milk at dinner or finger painting on the refrigerator with butter or trying to play a peanut-butter-and-jelly sandwich in the VCR. Remember the VCR? Modern families don't have to worry about that, but we did, and no, VCRs don't work after inserting a PB&J! When our kids spill their milk, they don't need a time-out or lecture; they need a towel. We need to overlook the small stuff, the broken stuff, the misplaced stuff, because it's all small stuff, and we don't need to whet the small stuff.

When your patience has faded and your frustration is running high; when you are at the end of your rope emotionally and want to explode, here are five parenting reminders from God's Word:

1. *When your child is angry,* remember: "A gentle answer will calm a person's anger, but an unkind answer will cause more anger" (Prov. 15:1, NCV).
2. *When you are frustrated with your child's behavior,* remember: "Losing your temper causes a lot of trouble, but staying calm settles arguments" (Prov. 15:18, CEV).

3. *When their room is not picked up,* remember: "Careless words stab like a sword, but the words of wise people bring healing" (Prov. 12:18, *GOD'S WORD*).

4. *When your child has failed,* remember: "Kind words are good medicine, but deceitful words can really hurt" (Prov. 15:4, *CEV*).

5. *When your child has been defiant,* remember: "Parents, don't be hard on your children. If you are, they might give up" (Col. 3:21, *CEV*).

There have been times when as a parent I have felt totally reactive instead of proactive, and like any normal parent, I have felt as if I am always on or always riding my kids about something. Focusing on the bad behavior instead of the good behavior is counterproductive. I realize that some days you really have to look for that silver lining—the one good thing they said or showed to you or to someone else, but don't forget that one good thing. Talk about it, reward it, highlight it, blog about it!

Because I really wanted to be proactive with our kids, and I want you to be proactive with your kids, I put together a reminder to say five simple things to them *daily*.

1. **D**o *your best.* ("So whether you eat or drink, or whatever you do, do it all for the glory of God" [1 Cor. 10:31]).

2. **A**lways *be thankful.* (Whatever happens, keep thanking God because of Jesus Christ. This is what God wants you to do [see 1 Thess. 5:18, *CEV*]).

3. **I** *love you.* ("Love never gives up, never loses faith, is always hopeful, and endures through every circumstance" [1 Cor. 13:7]).

4. **L**ove *God and others.* ("Love the Lord your God with all your heart, with all your soul, and with all your mind. Love your neighbor as you love yourself" [Matt. 22:37,39]).

5. **Y**ou *can do it.* ("I can do everything through Christ who strengthens me" [Phil. 4:13, *GOD'S WORD*]).

Whet Can You REPEAT This Week?

Great values are worth talking about and certainly worth repeating. The following schedule is designed to get your family talking and interacting together this week.

1. Monday
   Read the following verse out loud to your family: "Do not be misled: Bad company corrupts good character" (1 Cor. 15:33, *NIV*). "How important are friends when it comes to rude or respectful behavior?"

2. Tuesday
   Explain the importance of the following words: "I am sorry. I was wrong," "Please," "Thank you." Why are these words so important? What values are worth repeating in these words?

3. Wednesday
   Post this question on a large piece of paper: "How can we show respect and honor to one another?" Provide markers or crayons so that everyone can write more than one answer on the paper during the week. Discuss the question at the end of the day.

4. Thursday
   Encourage everyone in your family to pay it forward today. Example: If someone opens a door for you, open a door for someone else. If you are at Starbucks, pay for the drink of the person standing behind you. Then during dinner, discuss what happened that day. "What did you do to pay it forward today?" "What reaction did you get?" "How far do you think it went?"

5. Friday
   Ask each member of your family to notice every time someone is polite to him or her that day. Answer these questions over dinner: "Who treated you in a polite way today?" "What did that person do?" "What is another word for 'polite'?"

6. Saturday
   Take a survey at the end of the day by asking everyone what the best part of their week was.

It's exhausting to verbally and nonverbally repeat the behavior you want your children to demonstrate. As a reminder, look back at the four elements we talked about at the beginning of this chapter: Time, Skill, Patience and Understanding. When I look at those four words, I don't immediately think to myself, *How easy is this going to be? Patience and understanding are in my wheelhouse of traits I have mastered.* These things are not my strong points, especially when faced with a child who is ignoring me or being disrespectful or downright obstinate. But we as parents have to make a daily choice to repeat the right behavior to our children. If we do, our children will eventually make those choices too.

6

Reinforce the Behavior
You Want

Don't handicap your children by making their lives easy.
ROBERT A. HEINLEIN, *TIME ENOUGH FOR LOVE*

"My quiet, respectful, rule-following little angel has become a rude, pushy, aggressive little tyrant." Yes, I have heard a parent say that. What happened? The child grew up!

I can remember when I was about seven years old. We had a decent-sized back yard, a swing set, a few trees and a four-and-a-half-foot red-stained fence around the entire yard. The fence was there for a number of reasons but mostly for my mom's peace of mind. If I was in the fenced-in yard, she could run into the house for a minute and come back out without worrying about my behavior too much. The fence around our back yard kept me in a defined area. It was a visual limit, or border, for my world. I knew I couldn't go beyond the fence. I didn't know what was on the other side of the fence and didn't care. "Stay in the back yard" made sense to me, and I never challenged what my parents said . . . until I got a little taller.

The problems started as I went from three feet tall to five feet tall and could see over the fence. When my mom would say, "Stay in the back yard," I would now reply, "Why?" to which my mom would reply, "Because I said so." This conversation usually happens in every home when kids enter adolescence and push parenting to a completely different level. The "Because I said so" response isn't a bad response, and it isn't a bad way to parent your child—when he or she is very young. What's on the other side of the fence could be harmful or hurtful, and parents are simply protecting their children from that danger without giving an in-depth answer the children may not understand anyway.

When our children are younger, we usually parent by control. We tell our children to brush their teeth, take out the trash, turn off the TV, and when it's time to go to bed. We do most of this without a rebuttal or response from them. The tension comes when our kids change and we don't.

It almost seems as if when our children become teens, we become children. They have a new way of thinking and finding answers, challenging, pushing and questioning the limits of their world. They have grown tall enough to look over the fence to see what's on the other side; and if we haven't made a change in our parenting style when they ask to hop the fence, things will not go well. We will say no, and when they ask why, and we tell them, "Because I said so," we have a challenging opportunity on our hands. They have changed. And if we continue to parent by control, their behavior will most likely get worse, or they will totally shut down with us. What I am suggesting is that we can no longer parent by control; we must switch styles to match their new adolescent minds.

We need to be intentional in our parenting. As you go through this book, you will note that each chapter title offers a specific action we can apply as parents, and each chapter contains Bible verses that support the instruction and remind us of our role. Oftentimes when I read something helpful and practical, I highlight it but don't necessarily return to apply it. So I want to give you a little review to put all three chapters in this section into context, primarily to show how they are connected and that all three actions work together as a process. Take a look:

- Chapter 4: "Model the Behavior You Want"
  "You must love the LORD your God with all your heart, all your soul, and all your strength. And you must commit

yourselves wholeheartedly to these commands that I
am giving you today" (Deut. 6:5-6).
- Chapter 5: "Repeat the Behavior You Want"
"Repeat them again and again to your children. Talk
about them when you are at home and when you are on
the road, when you are going to bed and when you are
getting up" (Deut. 6:7).
- Chapter 6: "Reinforce the Behavior You Want"
"Tie them to your hands and wear them on your forehead as reminders. Write them on the doorposts of your
house and on your gates" (Deut. 6:8-9).

You probably noticed that this chapter, along with the previous two, is based on Deuteronomy 6:5-9. There is a relationship
between these verses that specifically emphasizes the need for
modeling and repeating and reinforcing. As a parent I am personally challenged by the three statements I wrote down in my
journal when I read these verses quite some time ago:

- "I can't model what I haven't practiced."
- "I can't repeat what I don't know."
- "I can't reinforce what I can't see."

I want you to pause for a moment before speeding through
this chapter to think about how each of the three chapters
of this section connects with the others. I wouldn't call the
relationship a step process where you first begin to model the
behavior; then you repeat it; then you reinforce it. It's more
organic than that, isn't it? The sheer weight of how to model
loving God with all my heart and soul and mind, and commit
to commands I might not even know, is enough for me to give
up immediately. If you find yourself in the same boat, grab
a paddle and take one stroke at a time and we'll eventually
get there.

Two Little Black Boxes

Deuteronomy 6:8-9 reads, "Tie them to your hands and wear them on your forehead as reminders. Write them on the doorposts of your house and on your gates." These verses are talking about a Jewish custom that involves small black boxes called phylacteries. The two little black boxes each hold four portions of Scripture written on parchment paper. The four scriptures were Exodus 13:1-10; Exodus 13:11-16; Deuteronomy 6:4-9; Deuteronomy 11:13-21.

Each phylactery was attached to the body with straps—one to the left arm and the other to the forehead—and worn during morning prayers. The location of each box was important. "The first phylactery was placed on the inside of the left arm, just above the elbow, so that the case would rest upon the heart. The phylactery was worn by every male over 13 years old at the time of morning prayer."[1]

The phylacteries and how they were used served as reminders of God's commands and care for the Jewish people. "The LORD told me [Moses] to give you these laws and teachings, so you can obey them in the land he is giving you. . . . You must always worship the LORD and obey his laws" (Deut. 6:1-2, CEV).

I can't help but think of how useful a tool this was (and is) for the Jewish people. I don't mean to demean the sacredness of the custom by calling it a tool. I understand the incredible symbolism and importance of the phylactery. They are a reminder of God's presence, love and promise. I see this as a healthy practice and routine that reminded and reinforced an attitude of hope and love for God.

Is it possible that a reminder can reinforce right behavior? I believe it can be. If we have been modeling the right behavior and repeating the right behavior, then we won't need to force the right behavior, just reinforce it.

Five Cs for Raising Polite Kids

1. Clarity

Setting clear boundaries in advance will help our children know where the line is. That does not mean they stay on the right side of the line;

it simply means they know where it is. They will not only push a boundary but also will exercise their will and cross it. If you haven't defined reasonable boundaries for your kids, how will you know what consequence to give once a line has been crossed?

I used to have these boundaries clearly defined in my head, but that meant no one else could see them. Now, we have several boundary lines written down! The list isn't long, and it's easy to remember. In fact, our kids, who are now teenagers, helped write the list and gave us the consequence for each boundary crossed!

If the lines are blurred, or there are no lines at all, you can't hold your children responsible for crossing boundaries when they don't know where they are.

2. Calmness

Remaining calm when our kids cross a defined line for the first time (or one hundredth time) is important. As our friend and marriage and family counselor Jim says, "Be aware of your emotions; don't act on them." Easy to say but hard to do. Respond but don't react. I will tell you there have been times as our kids got older when my emotions were running beyond capacity after they made a bad choice with their behavior. That's when I have needed to buy myself a little time, shift into neutral and let my emotions subside before they got the best of me. When I react, oh excuse me, over-react instead of respond, it rarely turns out well. There have been times when I have been so upset that I would have put all my kids on restriction until Jesus comes back. But that's an unhealthy reaction. It's hard to see the difference between healthy and unhealthy when emotions are running high.

Now that our kids are older, there have been occasions when Mary and I have put ourselves in "time out"! We have said these words to our kids: "We are going to take some time and process this together; if we don't take some time, we are going to make some choices that are not good for any of us."

3. Consequences

What is a consequence? Here's our definition: an appropriate result of something that occurred. The key word is "appropriate." Think back to what we just talked about: reacting, overreacting and responding. You want the consequence to match the inappropriate behavior. Let me give you an example.

One thing that often causes problems in our home is the beloved cell phone. In our family we have two boundaries regarding cell phones used by our children: (1) You may not bring your cell phone to the table, and (2) you must dock your cell phone in our room before you go to bed. The consequence for crossing either of those boundaries is cell phone related.

If one of our kids brings his or her phone to the dinner table, he or she loses the phone for the rest of the night. The phone is returned to the child the next morning. If he or she forgets to dock the phone before bed, that child loses the phone for the next day. Our entire family talked about the behavior, the boundary and the consequence, and we agreed on all fronts. Having our kids, as teenagers, be part of the process has made it easier and helped them understand the result of crossing a clearly defined boundary.

There are consequences for us as adults when we cross boundaries that have been clearly defined. That's just the way life works. Here is an example from my own life. In California, the speed limit on the 405 freeway is 65 miles per hour. That's a clear boundary. However, there have been a few occasions when I have crossed that boundary both unintentionally and intentionally. Unfortunately, I have not met one of my friends from the Highway Patrol who cared about whether I was intentional or unintentional about crossing the defined and posted boundary. I have a few "gift certificates" from my friends at the California Highway Patrol (two in one day), and the consequence appears to have a "range" in our beautiful state. From what I can gather, the range seems to be in the area of $250 to $500.

Now, I can choose to change my behavior by driving slower and staying within the posted boundary, or I can keep up my current behavior and get another gift certificate. (If you get several gift certificates within a certain amount of time, the consequences increase in "value.")

Let's revisit the cell phone example. If one of our kids forgets to dock his or her cell phone on Monday night, he or she gets the appropriate consequence—no phone the next day. If he or she forgets to dock it on Wednesday night, he or she gets the appropriate consequence. If it happens again and again and again . . . you can see where I am going with this. At what point is the child "forgetting" to dock the phone and "deliberately" choosing to not dock it for the night? Each family has to decide these matters, but at some point in our home, the consequences may increase.

Let's look at my real world "gift certificate" example for a moment. I may get one speeding violation, but if I get a few more, the consequences increase. In fact, I could end up losing my driving privilege because of my repeated behavior.

Mary and I have made the decision not to just give a consequence, but to connect the consequence with the rude or inappropriate behavior. If our children cross a boundary that has to do with their cell phone, the consequence will usually be associated with the further use of their cell phone. If they cross a boundary on Facebook, then the consequence has to do with the use of their Facebook account. We try our best to match the consequence to the behavior.

Take a look at the following list of inappropriate behaviors and the sample consequences associated with them. I am not suggesting that you immediately institute the following consequences for the associated behaviors; I simply want to show a connection between the behaviors and the consequences, as well as elevated consequences for repeated behaviors.

- **Inappropriate behavior:** disrespectful to parents
  Sample consequence: apologize correctly

- **Inappropriate behavior:** repeatedly disrespectful to parents
  Sample consequence: apologize correctly and write a letter of apology
- **Inappropriate behavior:** continued disrespect to parents
  Sample consequence: apologize correctly, write a letter of apology, loss of privileges
- **Inappropriate behavior:** playing a video game when told to stop
  Sample consequence: first conversation—lose game for the day
- **Inappropriate behavior:** continues to play video game when told to stop
  Sample consequence: second conversation—lose game for a week
- **Inappropriate behavior:** inappropriate texting
  Sample consequence: loss of phone for a week
- **Inappropriate behavior:** continued inappropriate texting
  Sample consequence: loss of phone for a month

Some parents might look at this list and say, "Are you kidding? My kids would get a much worse consequence for a few of the above-mentioned behaviors." I totally understand. There are also some parents who would read the list and say, "Are you kidding? How could you be so harsh on your children?" Again, I totally understand. There is so much to consider when correcting rude or downright inappropriate behavior. The situation, the circumstances surrounding the behavior and the personality of your child all come into play when seeking to correct behavior. Trying to prescribe only one method for your child or for mine is impossible.

Some children respond to that certain look you give them, and once they see that look, they may break down in tears, promising to never repeat the behavior again. They have a soft, tender spirit, and a small consequence goes a long way. Then there are other children who have a personality that dares you to do something about their behavior. These same children need to touch the stove to make sure it's hot. They are strong-willed, strong personality children. When you look at them with that certain parent look, they smile back at you with the "I dare you" look. As parents we need to think about how to parent each of our children the way *he or she* needs to be parented. A "one size fits all" parenting style rarely gives the best results—in fact, life experience has taught me that it can even be counterproductive.

4. Compliments

We must not get so focused on correcting our kids that we completely forget connecting with them. When your kids get it right, compliment them: "Great job!" "Well done, I knew you could do it!" "Great choice, I'm proud of how you behaved in that situation!" are all things we can and should be saying to our kids. We can occasionally get so stuck on correcting rude behavior that rude behavior is all we see. Tunnel vision isn't productive. In fact, it's harmful.

In 1902, sociologist Charles Cooley theorized the "looking-glass self." "In Cooley's theory of the 'looking glass self, [Cooley] states that our self-concepts and identities are a reflection of how other people perceive us."[2] While Cooley wrote about the theory in a general sense, there have been several studies conducted using the looking-glass theory within the context of family. The findings of one such study "suggest that how college students and adolescents think about themselves is directly correlated to how they think they are perceived by their parents."[3]

So, how important is it for kids to know how much we love and value them? As parents, we want to be the people who encourage and empower them! If we say to our kids things that are hurtful, harmful or hateful, we increase the chances that our kids will become those things. But if we parents allow grace, mercy, compassion and love to guide us in our most difficult and defining moments, I can't help but believe that our kids will be better for it.

5. Consistency

I can't tell you how important it is for both parents to be consistent and have their parenting styles aligned. Going to Dad to get one response but going to Mom when a different response is wanted is a child's version of divide and conquer. We can't let that happen. According to authors and counselors Drs. Les and Leslie Parrot, all couples fight over the same five things: "money, sex, work, parenting and housework."[4] They call them the big five! I'm sure you noticed number four on the list: parenting. So in order to stay on the same page and have a consistent response, here are three reminders.

1. Get on the same page before you open the book.

The solution for just about every parenting issue is to be on the same page, unified and of one mind. For some reason, kids are amazingly skillful at cracking that parental bond of solidarity. It's like they have studied it or taken a workshop on it. Soon, the behavior you intended to correct in your child ends up in an argument between you and your spouse while the kids watch the fireworks. There is a funny moment in an episode of the *Modern Family* TV series that sheds some light on the importance of parents being on the same page. Claire and her two daughters, Alex and Haley, are having a heated disagreement about whether or not Haley can go to a party for a couple of hours. Alex lets Mom know that her big sister was not studying the night before but was video chatting with friends the entire night. Claire tells Haley she cannot go to the party. The volume continues to escalate and Dad walks into the room.

> Phil: "Whoa, whoa, whoa, what's the hot topic on
>   *The View* today, ladies?"
> Haley: "Dad, can you just please tell Mom that I can take
>   a two-hour break and go to a party?"

Phil: "No,ma'am, I'm not stepping into that one. We're not playing 'good cop/mom'."[5]

What is not shown in this episode is the brutal argument that probably would have followed Phil's comment. In order to avoid the aftermath of a "good cop/mom" comment, we need to parent from the same perspective and support one another. It's hard enough being a parent. Why make an enemy of your spouse?

2. Don't undermine your spouse in front of your kids.

"Isn't that a little over the top?" "Don't you think you are over-reacting?" "I disagree with what you are saying to our kids right now." "Don't listen to your mom right now." "Don't tell your dad, but . . ." Don't let a comment that undermines your spouse's authority leak out in front of the kids. If something comes up that you haven't discussed or come to a decision on as parents, then call a time-out, move to a private area, discuss the options and return to talk to your kids with a unified decision.

3. Continue an open discussion on all parenting matters.

You don't have to wait until a crisis to talk about what you want to do or what you are going to do as parents. Having a continuing and open dialogue on what to do as parents or how parenting should be done is important because, as our children get older, our styles must shift. Remember, we move from control to influence so that our children can move from dependence to independence. While it may be easy to agree on the overall parenting philosophy, it may be tough to agree on the nuances of how we must change. For example, parents may agree on the idea of transitioning their parenting style to be one of more influence and less control in the teen years, but how much control to be given up in order to help the kids gain independence must still be determined. Keep the conversation going.

Four Areas Worth Understanding

1. The Influence of Good Friends

When I was a kid and would have friends from the neighborhood over to my house, my mom would always ask me questions about the friends when they left. I never knew why she did it until the reason occurred to me when I was a teen. She was screening my friends! She would talk to my friends and talk to their parents, not in an interrogative manner, but a friendly way. She would reach out and connect with them. She knew something very important about the power of friends and the power of influence. "Don't fool yourselves. Bad friends will destroy you" (1 Cor. 15:33, *CEV*). Choosing the right friends is one of the most important decisions we can make as adults, and which friends our kids have is especially important.

Looking back on my childhood, I would go so far as to say my mom selected my friends for me.

She never looked at a class or team picture and pointed out whom I could or could not hang out with, but she would always ask questions. "Tell me about Mike. What's he like in school? Who does he hang out with?" I never thought anything of it. Mom just knew. She was inquisitive but not invasive. That's how we need to be as our kids start choosing friends. Asking questions and showing interest in our kids' friends is a good thing to do, and "Who is . . ." and "Tell me about . . ." are great conversation starters.

The reason why choosing the right friends is so important is because of the natural process of friendships. First Corinthians 15:33 gives us a peek into the process when it tells us that bad company will ruin good behavior. Let me put it another way: If you go to a meeting and you are in perfect health, and you sit next to someone who has a cold, it is doubtful the person with the cold will catch health from you. It is more likely that you will catch a cold from the person who is sick. The same is true with friendship. If our kids choose the wrong friends or run with the wrong crowd, it is more likely that they will catch a character cold than a healthy attitude. Choosing the right friends is one of the most important decisions they will ever make.

2. The Power of Physical Touch

Paul Brand was the son of missionary parents and grew up in India until he returned to England for schooling. He eventually went on to become Doctor Paul Brand, a well-known orthopedic surgeon. He returned to India later in life with his wife, Margaret, to teach at a local hospital. It was during his time at the hospital in India that he saw the horrifying effects of leprosy that went untreated. One day at the hospital, "he gave a leprosy patient a friendly touch on the shoulder to assure him he would help him as much as he could. Tears started to stream down the patient's face, and Dr. Brand asked a colleague what he had done to distress him. She replied: 'You touched him, and no-one has done that for many years. They are tears of joy.'"[6]

It's hard for us to fathom the power of touch, because it's something we generally take for granted. Doctor Brand's story isn't the first time I have read about the power of touch. Let's look at two healing stories in the Gospel of Mark. The first healing is a story about a man who was paralyzed (see Mark 2). His friends brought him to see Jesus. The house was so crowded with people that the friends cut a hole in the roof and lowered their paralyzed friend right down in front of Jesus as He was teaching. Jesus simply looked at the man and told him to get up and go home! That's it! Get up and go home, and the man did. He walked right out of the house!

In Mark 1, we read another account where Jesus healed a man— a man with leprosy:

> A man with leprosy came and knelt in front of Jesus, begging to be healed. "If you are willing, you can heal me and make me clean," he said.

Moved with compassion, Jesus reached out and touched him. "I am willing," he said. "Be healed!" Instantly the leprosy disappeared, and the man was healed (vv. 40-41).

My question is simply, Why? Why touch the man with leprosy and not touch the man who was paralyzed? I believe Jesus touched the man with leprosy for the very reason Dr. Brand's patient started to cry. Neither of these two men—the one Jesus touched, and the one Dr. Brand touched—had been touched in a very long time. There is power in a touch. There is power when we put our arms around our children and hug them.

When our boys were born, our son Alec had to spend a few days in the NICU. During his stay, I found out something about the process of care for babies at this hospital. The hospital had a volunteer program called "snugglers." They are called snugglers because that is exactly what they do: they snuggle. They spend hour upon hour picking up babies in the NICU, sitting down in a chair and holding them. At the time, I thought the practice was a nice hospital amenity, but later I found out the research behind the power of touch in the NICU. "Benefits include stimulation of circulatory and gastrointestinal systems, better weight gain, lesser stress behavior, positive effects on neurological and neuromotor development . . . and improved sleep."[7]

Once while on a mission trip to an orphanage in Kazakhstan, our team walked into the nursery area to see several babies in their cribs, and most of them were crying. When one of the ladies on our team went over to touch one of the babies, she was stopped and told she could not touch them. I later found out from the orphanage director, through a translator, that if we touched the babies, they would become used to touch and cry louder when we left. They simply didn't have the staff to pick up every baby in the orphanage when he or she cried or needed something. As a result, no babies got touched when they cried.

If we gave each of our kids a loving and meaningful hug every day, I suspect that their self-esteem and self-confidence would improve. I believe that there is that much power in touch. Listen to what a good friend of mine told me in this regard:

Hopefully my story will help someone learn this the easy way and not have to go through what my wife and I did.

I'm a dad who likes to show affection, so with all three of our kids, I enjoyed wrestling, throwing them in the pool and rough-housing in general. Stephanie is our only daughter and our firstborn. We had a great relationship, and she was also very physical and loved to be swung and tossed. When she started looking and feeling like a young lady, the physical touching stopped, and I think it was mostly because I didn't want to do anything inappropriate or awkward. What I failed to realize was that this was the exact time when I needed to do just the opposite: to affirm her not only verbally but physically as well.

Stephanie interpreted my withdrawal as rejection, and our relationship went downhill fast. She has a strong personality and is not one to suffer in silence, so she became very outspoken and took it as her mission in life to reject us and everything we stood for, including our faith. This isn't just my opinion of what happened. Stephanie and I have talked about this now that she is an adult. She told me her rebelliousness and journey of rejection included multiple boyfriends, substance abuse and having a near-death experience from the choices she had made. She moved out of our home for 11 months when she turned 18, and there were many weeks when we didn't know if she was alive or who she was with.

I'm not blaming myself for her decisions, but I believe if I would have demonstrated my love and affirmed her during those fragile years when she needed it most, her story would have been different and most likely much less painful for all of us.

I only had brothers growing up and didn't really understand what girls went through. My wife told me that the junior high years were the worst for her for that same reason, but I didn't make the connection to our daughter, thinking that we had such a great relationship and that she was so confident (at that point) in who she was. I wish I could go back and make a few changes I know would have made a difference.

Showing physical affection to Stephanie by hugging her would have been the first change—a healthy and affectionate reminder that her father loves her and values her. I would have drawn her close, told her how unconditional my love is for her and how beautiful she is. If there was one thing I could tell each father of a daughter, it would be to hug her. Continue to show your affection for her. Tell her you love her. When you do, a healthy bond will be built that can never be broken.

3. The Value of Self-control

We like immediate rewards instead of waiting for better ones. We have a tendency to rush into decisions for the immediate pleasure rather than delaying our gratification for a later time. In his best-selling book *Emotional Intelligence,* Daniel Goleman discusses the battle between impulse and restraint, desire and self-control, ego and humility, and gratification and delay. One of the studies Goleman discusses had to do with four-year-olds and whether the choices made at that age had any effect later on in the lives of the children. The youngsters were given a "marshmallow test": the four-year-olds could, if they wished, eat a marshmallow immediately. Or, if they could wait until the tester returned, they would then be permitted to eat two marshmallows. Some four-year-olds, not surprisingly, grabbed the single marshmallow almost as soon as the tester left the room, while others—valiantly fighting off temptation—held out for 15 or 30 minutes until the tester returned, winning their well-earned two-marshmallow prize. All of the children were followed for several years, and the results were maybe not so surprising:

> When the two-marshmallow children were evaluated during their adolescence, they were measured against their one-marshmallow peers and found to be more confident, more competent, more assertive, more reliable, and less likely—when faced with difficulties—to quit, not to mention more eager to learn, better able to concentrate, and better able to achieve higher scores on the SATs. In addition, they continued to be far better at self-control.[8]

Helping our kids defer the immediate reward will help them as they mature into adults. The speed of life and our culture cater to the "If I want it now, I should have it now" mentality. Drive-through, fast food, Stop 'n' Go are all reminders that we can get in, get what we want and get out. Choosing good now, though, will remove the option of better at a later time. Teaching our children self-control and helping them delay gratification will give them a healthy process of behavior as they develop into mature adults. But modeling this behavior is the real key. For example, if you are a parent who shops until you drop, you will probably have a child who will cry until you buy.

What columnist Kathleen Parker has to say about boys applies equally well to girls:

> Reward good behavior, provide meaningful consequences for unacceptable behavior, make reasonable demands, express moral expectations, talk to their teachers and hug them every chance you get. Don't ask them to be

men when they are just little boys, but show them how to be real men by demonstrating the thing we as a society seem to have lost: self control. It's the greatest gift and it isn't even rocket science. It's just good parenting.[9]

4. The Process of Spiritual Growth

Ephesians 6:4 tells us, "Take them by the hand and lead them in the way of the Master." The reminder for us as parents is twofold. First, take them by the hand—guide them, direct them, show them the way. Second, we must know the way! When I was a children's pastor, there were two questions I would frequently hear parents ask that went something like this: "I don't know what to teach my kids about God. What steps should I take? Where should I start?" (Both are great questions, by the way.) So, to answer their questions, here are the four steps—*know, grow, serve, share*—that I would tell each parent to take, and I would tell them to start with the first step—*know*.

First Step to Know

Helping your child take his or her first step spiritually is really about introductions. I'm talking about introducing your child to God so that he or she knows who God is and comes to know Him in a personal way. "You have been taught the holy Scriptures from childhood, and they have given you the wisdom to receive the salvation that comes by trusting in Christ Jesus" (2 Tim. 3:15).

Next Step to Grow

The next step with your child on his or her spiritual journey is to help your child grow spiritually. This is about learning important habits like reading God's Word, having a quiet time with God, how to memorize a verse of Scripture and prayer. "But grow in the good will and knowledge of our Lord and Savior Jesus Christ" (2 Pet. 3:18, *GOD'S WORD*).

Step Up to Serve

When your child is growing in personal spiritual habits, it's time to help him or her understand the importance of serving God by serving others. Each of us has been shaped to serve God in unique ways. Helping your kids understand that we all have been equipped to serve others through our individual personalities, talents and experiences is a healthy step up in the right direction. "We should help people whenever we can" (Gal. 6:10, *CEV*).

Step Out to Share

Finally, your child needs to step out (this includes parents too) of their comfort zone and share their faith with others. This is not only important but also a command. The Bible says, "Go to the people of all nations and make them my disciples. Baptize them in the name of the Father, the Son, and the Holy Spirit, and teach them to do everything I have told you. I will be with you always, even until the end of the world" (Matt. 28:19-20, *CEV*).

In the back of this book, in the section titled "Additional Resources," there are four lessons you can teach your child (each lesson corresponds to one of the steps just mentioned) to encourage your child's spiritual growth. You can also visit whowillyou empower.com/steps for additional ideas and resources to help you in each of these four areas. I hope you will take that first step and begin to take your child by the hand and lead him or her in the way of the Master. You have heard it said, "The journey of a thousand miles begins with one step."[10] Those words are simple yet profound. The journey isn't easy; it's sometimes difficult, sometimes frustrating. But the journey is also rewarding, exciting and powerful.

The journey of a thousand miles seems like it will take forever; yet one day you will realize that you are on the last lap with your children. It won't be long before you will be attending their graduation, cheering them on in their first job, sitting in the front row of their wedding, holding your first grandchild. Time moves fast; it is relentless that way.

There are times on this journey when you will feel as if you have blown it as a parent. You have done your best and haven't seen any change in your children. Maybe you have been modeling the right behavior and repeating the right behavior for quite some time, but nothing seems to stick; you see no evidence of change. I want to encourage you to hang in there. The next few paragraphs on growing bamboo may give you some perspective on the process.

Raising Kids and Planting Bamboo

What I said earlier about self-control and delaying gratification goes for us as parents too. We can model the right behavior, repeat the right behavior, reinforce the right behavior, remind our children of what right behavior looks like and not see the results of our parenting immediately, or even for years. I'm sure we can all share a personal story or two about a time when we told our children, "Why did you do that? That's not how you were raised!" Well, if you are a parent who has thought such a thought and launched it in the direction of your child, wrap yourself in the confidence of the reminder from the book of James:

> My friends, be patient until the Lord returns. Think of farmers who wait patiently for the spring and summer rains to make their valuable crops grow. Be patient like those farmers and don't give up (Jas. 5:7-8, *CEV*).

In our modern world, we can get a lot of things in a hurry. But one thing we cannot get quickly is a mature adult from an immature child. Growth takes time and patience.

Those who plant Moso bamboo know all about patience. After a plant is placed in the ground, it can be two or three years before any visible growth occurs. The plant doesn't get taller. It doesn't flower. It doesn't send up new sprouts. There's nothing. Nothing visible anyway. Growth is happening, but it's happening underneath the soil.

It must be hard for those who care for this type of bamboo. They still need to care for the plant, water it, add fertilizer, tend the soil and protect it—all without seeing any results. Sound like parenting yet?

When Moso bamboo begins to grow, it grows rapidly. Some plants have been clocked, with a watch not a calendar, at a growth rate of nearly three feet in a 24-hour period.[11] Moso bamboo stocks have been known to top out at a height of 65 feet in 8 weeks. That growth rate feels a little bit like our children when they reach their teens!

The visible growth rate of Moso bamboo reminds me of how our children change and grow. Our children do grow up quickly, but sometimes it's hard to parent when you can't see any physical growth. When we don't see any growth in our kids, taking care of and tending to the needs and responsibilities we have as parents feels like all work, no reward. The reality is that there is tremendous growth happening, even though we can't always see the results.

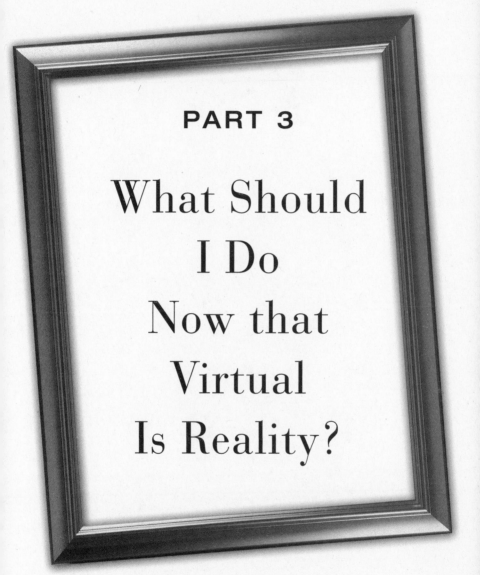

PART 3

What Should
I Do
Now that
Virtual
Is Reality?

7

Protect Your Child Online

www.whowillyouempower.com/protectonline

When I was a junior in high school, I was just like most high school students. I was struggling with my identity and self-esteem and trying to fit in. I came across tough enough and tried to look as if I had it all together, but one particular day, I got a lesson that would just about drive my self-esteem into the ground.

I was having lunch with a few of my usual group of friends just outside the cafeteria—a typical lunch—with everybody sitting in their usual spot. There were a few students causing trouble a few tables over, but that was typical as well. We were finishing up when I suddenly felt something hit my ear. It was a French fry. Usually, that would have been no big deal, and it probably shouldn't have been one then either; but as I looked around, I saw who threw it. Now, as a high school student who is trying to be accepted, act cool and fit in, what would you have done? Resist the temptation to take action or add fuel to the fire? I added the fuel by throwing another fry.

Everyone laughed, and I thought that was the end of it. Not quite. Another fry came my way, and I sent it back; then two fries, then three, back and forth until we both had run out of "fuel." Lunch was just about over, so everyone cleaned up and threw their trash away. I walked to my locker and as I turned around when I felt a tap on my shoulder, I was hit in the face, not with a fry, but with a fist. I couldn't even get my hands out of my jacket before the fight was over. There were maybe five people who watched me get humiliated that day.

This definitely had not been a good self-esteem-building exercise on two fronts: (1) I didn't even get my hands out of my pocket, and (2) other people saw it happen. I got hit, got hurt, got humiliated and went home. Notice the way it played out:

- I get hit.
- I get hurt.
- I get humiliated.
- I go home.

Today, it's different, much different. Today students of the same age I was are going through that same awkward stage of life where self-esteem is on the line, where they desperately want to be accepted. If the incident that happened to me were to take place today, it may start off the same way—a fry to the ear then a fist to the face. But what happens after that is radically different and only compounds the humiliation.

Notice how the incident would play out today, a time when the Internet is a part of the action:

- I get hit.
- I get hurt.
- I get humiliated.
- I go home.
- I get humiliated.
- I get humiliated.
- I get humiliated.
- I get humiliated.
- I get humiliated.
- I get humiliated.

Why the repetition of humiliation? Because someone recorded the fight on his cell phone and posted it online for the world to see. People who weren't even there can watch you get humiliated and then leave a comment on it as well. These days our kids are experiencing humiliation and low self-esteem in ways we never had to deal with when we were teenagers.

What happened to me—the bloody nose, the black eye, the feeling of being humiliated in front of five people—all of it faded away, and after a few days, no one could remember the fight at all.

Today, however, the same situation could be posted on the Internet, and the rest of the world invited to watch the humiliation. A black eye goes away; an online video does not. And it would probably go viral. Its repeated play (and resultant posted comments) leaves an emotional imprint on the child that can last a lifetime. Who wants their worst moments shared on social media? Kids today experience humiliation in ways we never had to deal with. That's why raising a healthy family in today's modern world requires open conversations with our kids about what goes on in the digital world.

Their Digital Community

When our boys turned 16, they wanted to have a party with some of their friends at a place called Howie's Game Shack—that place is loaded with computers and Xboxes and just about every game imaginable, as well as pizza and energy drinks. Our kids gravitate to Call of Duty and Halo. (No judging, please.) Mary and I dropped them off and watched as eight of their friends showed up for three hours of game playing.

When Mary and I returned to pick them up, this was the scene we saw: eight guys were seated side by side. All of them were staring at the same game, all of them wearing headsets equipped with microphones, and all of them were bobbing and weaving and laughing and yelling and having a great time.

If you were to look at that scene through (and I'm sorry if this stings a little) a pair of old-school glasses, you might be inclined to think these kids were all mindless students lost in cyberspace and not interacting with each other. Where is the community in that kind of behavior? Where is the conversation? Well, community is happening and conversation is happening; it's just not happening the way some of us did it. If you really look closely, you would notice that each of the students is a character in the game, and within the game there are two teams. They communicate with each other through the headsets and even strategize their next move as a group. Just because you and I did our strategizing with a stick in the dirt, and they do it with a controller and a headset, makes no difference when it comes to community.

Our kids are growing up in a time when things aren't always tangible, but they are readily available. Music, movies, grades, communication with friends—all are available through the air as they sit in a chair. This is their way, their life, their expression. We don't want to pull the plug on their connectivity; it's how they live. Imagine if your parents had taken away those lawn darts, wood-burning kit, erector set, tinker toys and Lite Brite! Painful, right! When those things were taken from us, we lost only one thing, something tangible. But when we take away our kids' connectivity, we are taking more than something tangible; we are taking their community. It's something to think about in our modern world. In fact, I would go so far as to say their community is much stronger for the sheer fact that each student can leave the game shack, go home and reconnect to their community when we could not.

Online gaming, social media, chat rooms, texting and most things media have made the world a more accessible and connected place. Most improvements in technology have impacted our world for the good. However, with new technology comes new responsibility, especially for today's parents. What do you need to know as virtual is reality for today's modern family?

Knowing what our kids are facing in today's world and how they interact digitally is important. When our children are in another room in the house, and they prefer that you text them instead of talk to them, virtual is your reality.

I can remember my mom telling me to never take candy from strangers and to never get in a car with anyone I didn't know; yet today's kids are taking digital candy from people they have never seen and getting into digital cars at an alarming rate.

- 71% of teens 13-17 say they received messages online from someone they did not know.
- 40% of those receiving messages said they usually reply and chat back.
- 30% of teens 13-17 have considered meeting someone they have only talked to online.
- 14% have actually had an encounter with someone they met online.[1]

After mentioning these statistics, I think it's good to remember Proverbs 22:6: "Direct your children onto the right path, and when they are older, they will not leave it."

It's safe to say that parents have a new role with their children in today's digital age. We must extend our parenting beyond the walls of what we can see and reach into the vast area of digital media, and that may require a little—or a lot—of learning on our part. If we are not familiar with the new media, then we are going to have to do some exploring and learning so that we can teach our children which path is the right one. That's my goal in this section. I don't want to force an opinion, although I will offer it occasionally as an example. I simply want to create awareness or a conversation about how we can raise a healthy family in a modern world.

Accessibility is the new normal. Pizza and pornography are equally accessible via smartphones, tablets and computers our children take with them to school. Sexting and cyber bullying have added new tactics and weapons to our enemy's arsenal.

When I wanted or needed information as a kid or as a teen, I had to buy a book or go to the library. Today, information isn't just available to our kids; it's injected, pressed and pushed into them, affecting their self-esteem and social perspective. Buying a book is something you do from your phone or tablet; libraries are turning into museums; and why would our children ask us about something they can get the answer to on Wikipedia? We parents need to not only get involved with digital media, but also get out ahead of the curve!

Change happens daily in the digital world. Our kids know this and understand it. Large companies know this and understand it and are taking advantage of it. So, if you still have a cord attached to your phone and you are still using a record player for your music (yes, I know vinyl sounds better), then it's probably time to start exploring your kids' new reality. You need to jump into the digital river that seems to be carrying our kids away without a paddle or life vest. Let me give you an example of something that recently happened to us.

A few months ago, when we received our cell phone bill we were shocked. It's usually the same price every month, but this month was different. It was several hundred dollars more than usual. When I started going through the bill, I noticed several charges for .99 cents. When I called our cell phone company to ask about the charges, they told me the charges were incurred from playing a game. Now here's the interesting part. My kids are on our cell phone plan, and each of them had downloaded a game to play on their phone—for free, I might add. As they play the free game, there are occasional messages that pop up on the screen asking what you want to do next or asking if you want to add anything to your game play. If you hit the wrong button (or the right button according to the game company), you continue on in the game and are charged a small fee. The fee is attached to your cell phone bill, and that fee is passed on to us as parents. Yes, it's legal, and no we didn't know that until we received the bill.

I know what you are saying: "Craig, take your kids off your cell phone plan; then you won't have to pay those fees!" But consider what would happen if I did that. The consequence to my children would affect me (and Mary) as well. I don't mean emotionally. What I'm thinking of are those times when you can't get ahold of them and it impacts you or your schedule. (I just wanted to see if you felt the same pain.) Now, I certainly understand your point about canceling our kids' cell phone service, but whether or not my kids are on or off my cell phone plan is irrelevant when they aren't old enough to get jobs. The bottom line is that I'm going to end up paying the cell phone bill no matter what. So, what's a parent to do? Get a longer reach!

Ten Ways to Extend Your Digital Reach

In today's world, you must extend your parenting into your kids' digital world. I like what Proverbs 27:12 says: "A prudent person foresees the danger and takes precautions. The simpleton goes blindly on and suffers the consequences."

Mary and I have started reading this verse a new way: "A prudent parent foresees the danger ahead and takes precautions. The simpleton parent goes blindly on and suffers the consequences." As parents, we need to see the dangers ahead, and we must take precautions.

What can you do to protect your child online? There are at least 10 things:

1. Use Internet filtering software on your computers.
2. Use parental controls on your computer and tablets.
3. Know your child's privacy settings on social media sites.
4. Spend time together with your child online.
5. Sign an Internet safety agreement with your child

6. Teach your child to never give out personal information.
7. Explain why your child shouldn't chat with anyone he or she doesn't know.
8. Discuss the appropriate use of the Internet with your children.
9. Show your child what to do if he or she stumbles onto inappropriate sites.
10. Frequently check your child's digital footprint.

Use of Internet Filtering Software

Your kids may not be looking for inappropriate content, but if they spend enough time on the computer, it will come looking for them. An ad or pop-up alert may get their attention, and before you know it, they are off and running. A simple Google search for a project they are researching for school may return a successful search for what they are looking for, but occasionally it will also include undesirable sites.

Even though your children's motives may be pure and healthy, they now find themselves faced with a decision. Do they continue with their school project or pursue their curiosity? Finish the research project or chase down a few links that sound pretty intriguing?

The way to get around that issue is to use Internet filtering or content control software on every computer in your home. With the most basic level, you can control what content is viewed online, and some software packages will send an email, text or alert to a specified email account or cell phone number so that you are kept aware of what is happening or has happened on one of your home devices.

Here are three Internet filtering software options:

1. *Bsecure*—Endorsed by Focus on the Family, Bsecure (www.Besecure.com) provides social networking protection, online media filtering, and text and email alerts to parents' phones.

2. *Social Shield*—Offering you a total view of the social networking your kids are doing, SocialShield (www.socialshield.com) will alert you to potential dangers and will give you information to keep your children safe and protect them online.

3. *Safe Eyes*—An award-winner, Safe Eyes (www.internetsafety.com) will make you aware of content that is being accessed and other dangers that pose a threat to your children on the Internet.

When you are looking for Internet filtering software, consider one that covers your mobile devices as well. (Smartphones and tablets are the new normal and need to be filtered.)

Use of Parental Controls on Computers and Tablets

Parental controls differ from filtering software in that you can regulate screen time as well as block sites and record what content your kids are viewing or trying to view on one computer in your home. Both PC and Mac computers have built-in parental control screens that allow you some control over the use of the computer.

The parental controls on the Mac computers at our home are very intuitive and allow us to set not only the amount of screen time available to our kids each day but also what time of the day the computer can be used. The Mac controls also allow us to see all sites that have been viewed, or attempted to be viewed, without allowing the user to delete the browser history. You have to understand that your children may actually be smarter than you when it comes to using a computer, and they may be able to mask or cover up their digital footprint after they have finished using the computer. Certain parental controls, however, allow you to capture that information.

The Internet is a powerful resource for us and for our children, but when using the kind of power the Internet gives us, we need to remember the words of Luke 12:48: "When someone has been given much, much will be required in return; and when someone has been entrusted with much, even more will be required." We must do all we can to keep our children safe, protected and accountable.

Use of Privacy Settings on Social Media Sites

Before your kids jump on the social media highway, you should prepare them for the occasional emotional fender bender that will undoubtedly accompany them on their journey. That being said, there are a few things you can do to minimize their accident risk as they drive along their digital highway.

At what age should children be allowed to have a social media page? Here are the current minimum age requirements for a few of the most popular social media services and applications:

- You must be 13 before creating an account on Facebook.
- You must be 13 before creating an account on Instagram.
- You must be 17 before creating an account on Vine.
- You must be 13 before creating an account on YouTube.
- Currently, there is no minimum age for a Twitter account.

Just because your children meet the minimum age requirement does not mean they are ready for social media. Is each of your children emotionally mature enough to have a social media page? Do your children understand the benefits associated with social media? Do they understand the risks of these sites? In my opinion, the benefits far outweigh the risks in having a Twitter, Facebook, Instagram or whatever comes next account. But just like anything in this world, the benefits only outweigh the risks if they know how to safely use it.

Once your children join a social media site, the first thing they should do is send you a friend request. You will want to be a part of their social media circle, not necessarily as a participant, but certainly as an observer. I can remember when I was in high school, I asked my mom if she could drop me off around the corner so I could walk the rest of the way so that I wouldn't be embarrassed by the other kids seeing me with my mom. All kids are different; some go through that embarrassment phase, and some don't. If your children are like I was, they may be embarrassed that you are their "friend" online, but that's okay. Hold your ground and make sure you are part of their online social circle. (By the way, I was never dropped off around the corner; and although I felt embarrassed, I never was embarrassed by my mom.)

Thinking back to the unconnected world I was born into, I can remember getting three presents for Christmas one year. When I was seven, I got a Lite Brite, a wood-burning kit and lawn darts. You may already know where I am going with this. But let me explain. Two out of three of those presents could kill you or at the very least give you a large sized flesh wound.

In today's world, you would never think of giving your seven-year-old three "spears" with instructions that told him to go outside and "toss in the air" to play! And, it was probably good that we didn't have any pets in our home during the "wood-burning kit years" or there would have been a few branded animals in our home. To be honest, I am surprised I didn't set fire to the house! However, I do live with a few scars on my hands from where I misused the toy. (Imagine, a kid with ADD and lawn darts!) Here's my point: Giving your children access to something they are not ready for may not be the best choice. Social media sites can be great if used respectfully and responsibly. Knowing your child's privacy settings on these sites will help them learn respect and responsibility within healthy boundaries.

Reflecting back on my seven-year-old Christmas, the reason I didn't get hurt or hurt someone else with those "lawn weapons" was because I was supervised when I was playing with them. The reason I didn't burn down the house with the wood-burning kit was because I could only use it when my parents were present. My parents had settings for me; they had boundaries. The boundaries were there to protect me—to protect me from myself and from hurting others. Today the illustrations have changed, but the parental responsibility remains the same. Know your child's social media privacy settings.

The sample social media agreement we used with our kids when they were younger and just getting started on the social media highway is at the back of this book (see the "Rules for Maintaining a Healthy Social Media Account" in the Additional Resources section). To view the agreement online, go to http://www.whowillyouempower.com/protectonline. (See graphic on the next page.)

Spend Time with Your Child Online

Sit down with your children and spend some time with them on-line—showing them and modeling for them how to use cyberspace in a healthy way. Talk about what they should do if something inappropriate comes up on their screen. You don't want them to hide anything from you, and you don't want them to cover their digital tracks. By spending time together with your children online, you can help them understand the importance of exploring a healthy digital space.

Make an Internet Safety Agreement with Your Child

I know that not all parents like using behavioral contracts or agreements with their kids, but in regard to protecting your children on the Internet, I'm not so much pushing a contract as I'm talking about accountability. Whether it's a contract or agreement you sign, or a set of reminders you post on a wall where your kids can see them, the point is that you and your children share and follow a set of expectations of how to responsibly use the Internet. A sample "Internet Safety Agreement" is available for you to use (see the Additional Resources section at the back of this book, or go online to http://www.whowillyouempower.com/protectonline). (See graphic on page 151.)

Protect Personal Information

Free! That's the word. It's captivating. It's intriguing; and it's free! Usually, sites that are trying to get information start by asking a

Rules for Maintaining a Healthy Social Media Account

1. You must "friend" Mom and Dad and keep us as "friends" at all times.
2. You must provide your social media password to Mom and Dad and let us know if you ever change it.
3. Do not "friend" anyone that you don't know personally. For example, don't "friend" another person's friend just because you know that other person.
4. Don't post a profile picture with someone other than a best friend, family member or pet. At some point your girlfriend or boyfriend is acceptable.
5. Don't "like" or comment on any post that will hurt someone else, hurt your parents or disappoint God.
6. Don't post any pictures of others without their permission—including a profile picture. Ask them first.
7. Don't "like" any websites, apps, music or videos that are inappropriate. If you don't know, then ask Mom or Dad.
8. Remember that future employers and universities often check social media sites when considering you for employment or enrollment when you are older.
9. Ask Mom and Dad if you have any questions or concerns about something on any social media site.
10. Think before you post anything. Things you post can exist forever online, even if you delete them right away. Someone could have taken a screen shot of your post and saved it. If you are not sure if you should post something, *don't* post it.

I understand these social media guidelines, and I also understand that if I break one of these rules my account(s) may be suspended as a consequence.

Child's Signature: _____ Today's Date: _____
Parent's Signature: _____ Today's Date: _____

simple question. Maybe it's your first name, your age, or the last grade you completed in school. This may be followed up by a few more seemingly innocuous questions, like the name of a favorite animal or the name of a pet. To a savvy marketer, all information

CRAIG JUTILA

can be used to gain ground into the lives of your children—or of you as a parent, for that matter.

Continue to remind your children that when they are online, they are not to give out any personal information, for any reason, at any time. This applies to the personal information of other people as well. When someone on a social media site asks your children about their friends, your children should be taught to say, "I don't know; why don't you ask them personally?" Go over with your children examples of personal questions: "Where does your mom work?" "Are your parents at home right now?" "What school do you go to?" These questions are all examples of personal information that should not be given to an unknown person.

Online with an Unknown Person

It's a shame that you have to do this, but explain to your children that there are people who hide behind the anonymous mask of the Internet. Explain that just because someone says her name is Tiffany and appears to go to their school doesn't mean that it's really Tiffany at the other end of the chat.

Online gaming with an Xbox or PlayStation is a bit more difficult to deal with. When our kids played online group games that involved players from around the world—all chatting and talking together during game play—we would simply have them play with the sound on so we could hear the conversation. It's safe to say that our values as a family are not always the same values of other families. With that said, how do you respond to a few four-letter words that are dropped throughout the game? Do you have a strict "Turn that off" policy? At a certain age, we did.

However, as our kids got older, we decided to help them navigate their world by asking them questions: "What did you think about that guy's language?" "Why do you think they use that language?" "Why do you think that gal was threatening the other player during the game?" Giving our children this additional freedom not only built trust between us but also helped them to

Internet Safety Agreement

I promise to never give anyone my personal information or information about my family when I am online. Examples of my personal information include my name, age, address, telephone number, school or passwords.

I promise to never write anything mean or post any picture or video that hurts, humiliates or makes fun of others.

I promise to let my parents know if someone sends me a mean message and I promise not to respond to it.

I promise to only talk, text or chat with people I know and of whom my parents have approved.

I promise to always ask my parents before joining any site, club or social media site.

I promise to not click on any advertisements that may pop up on my screen or come to me in an email.

I promise to always tell my parents if I find anything that makes me uncomfortable while I am on the Internet, such as bad words, pictures or videos that make me afraid or uncomfortable.

I know that my parents will be checking my Internet steps and other digital places I visit to keep me safe.

Child's Signature: _____ Today's Date: _____
Parent's Signature: _____ Today's Date: _____

think through and develop their own healthy online boundaries. We want our kids to know that we know what goes on when they play online. This has allowed open conversations about the best way to navigate this aspect of their digital world.

CRAIG JUTILA

Appropriate Use of the Internet

Why do your kids use the Internet? To study? To play? To interact? Yes! It's a one-stop shop, isn't it? Some people may say, "Craig, you are harshing my digital world. Why are you so negative about the Internet?" Easy answer: I'm not! I love the Internet. As an author, it has made my life easier in a hundred different ways—the two most important being research and accessibility to content. Not too long ago, I would have had to go to the library and use the card catalog (remember that?) to look up a book or author. Research was legwork; now it's finger work. So no "harshing" here, just a few thoughts about how to appropriately use this amazing tool. And, IMHO (in my humble opinion), studying, playing and interacting are all great uses of the Internet.

How to Deal with Inappropriate Websites

As you spend time online with your children, help them understand what they should do if they stumble upon something inappropriate. When they start using the Internet, most kids don't go looking for inappropriate sites or content, but they may either stumble on it while at home or see it while at the home of one of their friends who decides to show everyone else what he or she has found.

If your children are at a friend's home when the inappropriate content comes up on the screen, they may stay and watch because they are afraid of being ridiculed or harassed if they were to stand up and walk out of the room. Peer pressure can overwhelm their sense of what's right. If your children have faith in Christ, they will also have to deal with the guilt of viewing the content as well as the guilt of not telling you about it. It's important to have early and open conversations with your kids about what to do when—not if—they come across unhealthy content on the Internet. Keeping open communication between you and your children is extremely important, and it's something I haven't always done well. I had to make a conscious effort to move from a lecture style of parenting to a listening style, especially as my kids have gotten older.

Awareness of Your Child's Digital Footprint

What's a digital footprint? A digital footprint is similar to a regular footprint, which is simply an impression or mark you leave as you physically walk around. In this case, it's a mark you leave as you digitally walk around. A footprint usually tells you a few things. First, it will always tell you where you have been. And second, it usually tells you where you are going. I believe that frequently checking your child's digital footprint is a step in a healthy direction.

What about respecting your child's privacy? We will take a deeper look at that in the next chapter. For now, let me just say that while I agree that a certain amount of privacy is essential for your child's growth, maturity and healthy independence, I feel it would be parentally irresponsible to not check your child's digital footprint on a regular basis. Remember what the Proverbs verse said about being prudent as we look ahead, not regretful as we look back. Filtering out unwanted content from your eight-year-old son's browser or blocking certain social media sites for your nine-year-old daughter may be something you find not only useful but also absolutely essential as kids engage this modern world their way.

The leadership wisdom from the tribe of Issachar, found in 1 Chronicles, is a good reminder for us: "From the tribe of Issachar, there were 200 leaders of the tribe with their relatives. All these men understood the signs of the times and knew the best course for Israel to take" (1 Chron. 12:31). How did the leaders know the best course to take? They understood the times in which they lived. They not only knew the culture, but they also knew how to navigate it.

If we read this verse in the context of parenting, it may read, "Every parent understood the signs of the times and, as a result, knew the best course of action to take with their children." Wow! How powerful is that? Can you imagine the insightful ways that we could apply modern-world technology for the better if we really understood the times in which we live? Understanding will lead to wisdom—if you let it.

8

Set Digital Boundaries

www.whowillyouempower.com/digitalboundaries

Due to inappropriate use of media by children while on campus, a middle school principal sent the following email to the parents of the school children because he wanted to encourage parents to check their child's media access:

Dear Parents,

I am sending this out to all of you to make you aware of an issue that is becoming more of a concern in all middle schools. Since our return from winter break we have had multiple issues concerning social networking that I want you to be aware of including: students posting images of other students, writing inappropriate comments, posting videos, bullying, etc. These all have an effect on student safety. I am asking all of our parents for support in this matter by taking a few minutes this weekend to have a conversation with your child about social networking and their use of it.

The principal was giving the parents excellent advice. You have to realize that there are numerous free online resources that your children may be accessing, with or without your knowing it, including but not limited to the ones I've already mentioned: Instagram (photo feed), Facebook (social networking), Flickr (photo streaming), YouTube (video sharing), Vine (video sharing), Twitter (social networking/microblogging), Tumblr (social networking/microblogging), Kik (free texting/insta-messaging), Snapchat (photo messaging), videos and drawings, Skype (free Internet calls), Facetime (video calls), OoVoo (free video messaging), voice and instant messaging. The days of parents just needing to check their children's email or Facebook page are over; there are new social sites created every day. I loudly echo what a friend wrote to me:

> It is important to talk to your child about the sites listed above and also to monitor your child's cell phone, iPod, tablet, computer, etc., and to please continue to remind your child that whatever is posted online, even for just a second, can be very permanent and travel quickly around the world. Even though a child may think they can simply "delete" what they have posted . . . it is not that simple. Once something has been posted online, it may be in the hands of one or more persons forever.[1]

The reminder for me in this email is that there are numerous free online resources that your child may be accessing, with or without your knowing. As my daughter would say, "Tru that!" If your children have a mobile device that can connect to the Internet, they can connect with or without your approval. This is another reason to explore Internet filtering software compatible with mobile device operating systems.

Two verses come to mind as we talk about setting digital boundaries for our children. The first is Proverbs 22:3 and the second is Proverbs 27:12. Although we discussed Proverbs 27:12 in the previous chapter, there's a reason I want to repeat it here: There is something unique about these two verses. See if you can find it.

> A prudent person foresees danger and takes precautions. The simpleton goes blindly on and suffers the consequences (Prov. 22:3).

> A prudent person foresees danger and takes precautions. The simpleton goes blindly on and suffers the consequences (Prov. 27:12).

I hope you saw what was unique about these two verses. Any similarities? LOL. They are not only similar—they are identical! If you have two verses that repeat themselves, it may be worth our attention. (As a sidebar: To those who say the Bible is not relevant in today's world, excuse me for a moment while I get my soapbox. Okay, now that I have it, let me say that it's amazing how relevant the Bible is for today's modern family! These two verses fit hand in glove to the topic we are talking about in this section.) Simply put, we need to be prudent parents.

Back to School

Before we look at setting a few digital boundaries for our children, here's a little bit of background to better understand what we're dealing with. To do that, we must head back to school for a brief lesson. Are you ready?

1. Hebrew Language

The word "prudent" in the Proverbs verses we just read is a Hebrew word, *arum*.[2] English synonyms for the word *arum* would be "crafty, shrewd, or sensible."

2. Fun Fact

That same word, *arum,* is used in Genesis 3:1: "Now the serpent was more crafty than any beast of the field which the Lord God had made" (*NASB*). See that word "crafty"? It's the word *arum.*

3. English Lesson

Do you remember learning about subjects and predicates in sentences when you were in school? Me neither, so let me give you, and me, a brief recap. Every complete sentence contains a subject and a predicate. The subject is the "what" or the "who" of the sentence, and the predicate tells us something about the subject. Now, hold that thought for a moment.

4. History Lesson

The Old Testament was originally written in Hebrew. When the Old Testament was translated into Greek, it was called the Greek Old Testament, or the Septuagint. The reason for the history lesson is the word *arum.* When *arum* was translated from Hebrew into Greek, *arum* became the word *panourgos,* which means "cunning, crafty, skillful and clever." A literal translation of the word would be, "a person doing anything to get his way (anything it takes)."[3]

5. Greek Language

In the New Testament, the word *panourgos* is only used in 2 Corinthians 12:16: "But be that as it may, I did not burden you myself; nevertheless, crafty fellow that I am, I took you in by deceit" (*NASB*).

6. Context

When you read Genesis 3:1, recall the subject/predicate lesson. You will notice the subject is the serpent, who is Satan. The predicate is crafty. When you read 2 Corinthians 12:6, the subject is "I" or Paul, who was the writer. The predicate is crafty. Both uses of this word are in a negative context. In both cases, it is by cunning deceit or clever trickery that the subjects of the sentences got what they wanted. At this point, you may be saying to yourself, *Craig, I don't think you are making the point you think you are making.*

7. Bringing It Home

The Hebrew or Greek word for "prudent" doesn't change its meaning in these two Scripture examples. It still means "cunning, crafty or clever." The context in which the word is used is of someone who is less than honest in his or her behavior. I wanted you to see the interchangeability of the word or words as we think about setting digital boundaries for our children. If we were to take what we now know from our seven steps and paraphrase the verses in Proverbs about prudent parents, they might read something like this.

> A smart parent will look ahead a few years and see the hazards and traps that are waiting for our children in this modern world. So, with all the shrewdness of a stockbroker and the cunning of a fox, and with all the cleverness of a cat burglar, be sensible and use your skill to protect your children online. If you look the other way for a while, hoping things will naturally improve, they won't, and you will suffer as a result.

Parents, we must provide our children with what they need to navigate their modern world in a healthy way. There is a Spanish proverb that says, "What a fool does in the end, the wise do in the beginning."[4] So with that in mind, let's take a look at six digital boundaries we can prudently set for our children for their own good.

Six Digital Boundaries to Protect Our Children

Following this numbered list is an overview of what each suggestion means along with information to help and encourage you as you set healthy digital boundaries for your child.

1. Keep computers, tablets and game consoles in an open space.
2. Set appropriate limits for daily screen time.
3. Children must not sign up for anything unless they get permission.
4. Charge mobile devices in an open location overnight.
5. When family time is on, all media is off.
6. Randomly check your child's texts.

Keep Computers, Tablets and Game Consoles in an Open Space

It's less likely that your children will explore inappropriate content if their screen is in a spot where everyone can see it. As I researched this topic—from using Facebook posts to asking other families—I thought Mary and I would be in the minority in setting this boundary. However, most websites I checked included this specific digital boundary, including sites like MTV and ABC. At Findlaw.com, the recommendation is listed as a suggestion, but also as something you should do for kids ages 7-18.

Set Appropriate Limits for Daily Screen Time

Notice the suggestion is for screen time, not computer time. Screen time is *anything* with a screen—game console, TV, computer, smartphone, tablet, etc. How much time is enough time? It really is up to each individual family. The older our kids get, the more homework needs to be completed and emailed or filled out online. As the world progresses, I'm sure we will use less paper and more digital modalities: quizzes taken online, tests taken in class on an iPad, projects completed and emailed. Honestly, it makes sense to me. I like and embrace the digital direction we are going.

As adults, we may be aware enough to remove ourselves from the screen for a few moments and unplug from the media. However, I must admit that while writing this book, my eyes have, on occasion, started to burn to the point of having to stop and put in a few eye drops. Studies show us that our blink rate dramatically decreases when we are on the computer, producing what ophthalmologists call dry eye. One such study "measured the blink rate of 104 office workers. The average blink rate was 22 blinks per minute under normal conditions, 10 blinks while reading a book and only 7 while viewing text on a computer."[5]

Screen time can become an addiction if not regulated. To the teenager who is connected to friends online, it can be difficult to unplug for a few moments. They have a deep desire to know what's going on with their friends and in their world. To be offline for a few minutes risks being out of the loop or forgotten. At the very worst, if they are offline, they risk invisibility or becoming irrelevant in their social circles.

Taking periodic breaks from the screen is helpful for all of us, not just for our kids. Here are three important things we *can't* do while staring at a screen.

1. Be Still

I am not talking about sitting down. I am talking about being still in your heart, mind and emotions, which is unlikely if you are engaged in front of a screen. Nicholas Carr, bestselling author on technology and culture, has this to say:

> Media aren't just channels of information. They supply the stuff of thought, but they also shape the process of thought. And what the Net seems to be doing is chipping away my capacity for concentration and contemplation.[6]

> I often feel as if I have been trained by the Internet to remain mentally active and emotionally impatient when offline and sitting still. I fully expect to take in all my information and experiences in short frequent bursts, and I occasionally get restless and agitated when sitting still.

A verse like Psalm 46:10 can serve as a reminder to cultivate stillness: "Be still, and know that I am God." Or as Job 37:14 says, "Stop and consider the wondrous works of God" (*ESV*). When we are in front of our screens, research suggests that we are constantly active.

> When we go online, we enter an environment that promotes cursory reading, hurried and distracted thinking, and superficial learning. It's possible to think deeply while surfing the Net but that's not the type of thinking the technology encourages and rewards.[7]

2. Be Quiet

"Whenever we turn on our computer, we are plunged into an 'ecosystem of interruption technologies,' as the blogger and science fiction writer Cory Doctorow terms it."[8]

It's hard to be quiet in the midst of noisy interruptions.

3. Listen

When we are online, we are often oblivious to everything going on around us. The world seems to fade into the background of whatever we are watching, doing, or interacting with on screen. When I am online, staring at the screen, I can usually hear what is going on around me, but I am not listening to what is going on around me. My wife tells me there is a big difference between hearing and listening. (She is a speech pathologist and somewhat of an expert on the topic.) She tells me the main difference between hearing and listening is attention.

She says that hearing is a passive physiological response to outside auditory stimuli—an alarm clock, a car idling, a bird singing, the barista making my grande nonfat caramel macchiato. You don't have to focus to hear; you don't have to pay attention to hear the sounds around you.

Listening, on the other hand, is an active behavior and requires focus. Active listening means that everything—your eyes, ears, mind, heart and soul—is engaged, and you simply cannot do this while parked in front of a screen. Let's take it a step further. What must we do to hear a whisper? I would say, based on what Mary told me, I would need to eliminate all distraction and hyper focus on what was being communicated. It just so happens that the Bible talks about how God sometimes talks to us: "And after the earthquake there was a fire, but the LORD was not in the fire. And after the fire there was the sound of a gentle whisper" (1 Kings 19:11).

While observing a few interactions in our own home the other day, I wrote down a few things you must do in order to hear someone whisper:

• Stop what you are doing.
• Face the person who is whispering.
• Lean in.
• Concentrate.
• Block distractions.
• Engage your mind (try to understand what the speaker means).
• Engage your heart (try to understand what the s peaker feels).

If we want to hear God, if we want our families to hear God, we need to be active listeners. We simply can't listen to God or our family when we are staring at a screen. Setting healthy boundaries on screen time will add value to your family life.

Children Must Not Sign Up for Anything Unless They Get Permission

This point seems logical enough, but there are so many creative ads and product placements in the media that it's hard to know which ones are for legitimate companies.

As I've mentioned before, it is an unfortunate fact that unscrupulous people often masquerade behind what appears to be something legitimate in order to gain information they can use to gain access to your children or to you for the purposes of identity theft. "In 2010, 7.0% of households in the United States, or about 8.6 million households, had at least one member age 12 or older who experienced one or more types of identity theft victimization."[9] Identity theft continues to be one of the fastest growing crimes today. Simply be aware, and help your children understand the importance of having parent permission before they sign up for anything.

Charge Mobile Devices in an Open Location Overnight

Requiring that all mobile devices be charged in one open location overnight is actually a habit that contributes to good health.

A friend of mine was telling me about the moment he and his wife started to implement this strategy. While checking his cell phone bill one day, he noticed there was a very large increase in texts sent and received. Most of us have unlimited texting on our phones, and if you do have that type of plan, then you will rarely if ever see an increase in your bill. He noticed that the texts were between the hours of 11:00 P.M. and 2:00 A.M. Apparently, late-night texting had been going on for a while.

There was nothing inappropriate in the texts, but his thought—and mine—was, *Why do you need to be texting between the hours of 11:00 P.M. and 2:00 A.M.?* High school love? I get it. I married my childhood sweetheart. Of course, we had no cell phones, so we had to be creative when it came to the idea of "I want to let you know I am thinking about you, but I don't have the ability to send words over the air while I am sitting in my room because it's the 1980s" theme. So I would go to the kitchen, pick up the phone, dial Mary's number, let it ring once and then hang up. When Mary would hear the one ring, she knew it was me; she knew I was thinking about her, and that was it.

To be fair, her parents didn't like the one ring at midnight. I honestly hadn't thought it through. Our kids, as hard is it may seem, may not always think through what they are doing. Texting a boyfriend or a girlfriend in the middle of the night is not a life-or-death scenario, but inadequate sleep can be detrimental to your children's health. Having your children dock and charge their cell phones in your room or another room of the home will go a long way at preventing sleepless nights.

When Family Time Is On, All Media Is Off

I say "media off" during family time with a little leeway. If your family time consists of doing something online or requires the use of your cell phone, like geocaching, then yes, keep on as much media as you need. My suggestion here is meant to prevent anyone in your family from texting or checking his or her individual social media statuses while you are having uninterrupted family time together.

There is also quite a bit to be said about being together as a family and having *no* cell phones on at all. Remember chapter 3, the section about good, better, best? I actually have a specific family time I am thinking about: dinner together as a family. When having dinner with your family, my suggestion is to disconnect digitally and rewire relationally. You can do this by eliminating all digital distractions and focusing on face-to-face conversation. (Oh, and if you are having a difficult time getting the conversation going at dinner, go back to chapter 5 under the heading "Whet the Entire Family with Five Routines—3. Eating Together" and use one of the 31 ways to finish a sentence to get your family talking.)

Having "unplugged" dinner together isn't the be all and end all answer for a healthy modern family. Some families can't have dinner together due to work or school schedules. In those cases, "dinner together" could mean breakfast together, time in the park together, a ride in the car together. However, keep in mind that if you want to get the biggest benefit over time, when your family is on, all media is off.

Randomly Check Your Child's Texts

One of the ways we protect our children is by randomly checking their texts. This is a boundary that is tricky, because it involves privacy. If you're interested in a possible way to avoid at least some cell phone problems, consider signing a cell phone responsibility agreement with each of your children. (See the "Cell Phone Responsibility Agreement" in the Additional Resources at the back of this book for a sample or go online to http://www.whowillyouempower.com/protectonline to download a copy.)

Cell Phone Responsibility Agreement*

Normal Use
- ❑ I will not text or place phone calls between ___:___ P.M. and ___:___ A.M.
- ❑ I will send no more than _____ texts per day.
- ❑ I will not exceed my allotted monthly minutes or text message limits.
- ❑ I will charge my phone in an open space and not in my room.

Safety
- ❑ I will answer my phone when my parent calls.
- ❑ I will not download/subscribe to anything on my phone without parental permission.
- ❑ I will not disable any parental controls on my phone.
- ❑ I will tell my parents when I receive inappropriate texts or sexts.
- ❑ I will tell my parents if I am being harassed by someone on my cell phone.
- ❑ I will not harass or bully anyone with my cell phone.
- ❑ I will not use my cell phone to arrange meetings with anyone my parents don't know.

Texting
- ❑ I will not send threatening or mean texts to others.
- ❑ I will not take or send embarrassing photos of myself, my family or my friends.
- ❑ I will not share photos with other people without their permission.
- ❑ I will not text messages about people in a way that hurts their reputation.
- ❑ I will not forward a hurtful message or picture sent to me about someone else.

Being Polite
- ❑ I will not bring my cellphone anywhere that my parents prohibit its use, like the family dinner table.
- ❑ I will not be rude to others by talking or texting in public places where cell phone use is not allowed or is inappropriate, like in a church or a library.
- ❑ I will follow all school rules about cell phone use.

The following are reasonable consequences if any of the above rules are broken.

Consequences
- ❑ I understand that having a cell phone is a privilege that can be taken away.
- ❑ I understand this agreement will help me to demonstrate responsible behavior.
- ❑ I understand my parents reward good behavior with more freedom.
- ❑ I understand there are consequences for breaking this agreement.

Parent Responsibilities
- ❑ I will answer any questions my child has about owning a cell phone.
- ❑ I will periodically revisit these rules as my child gets older and technology evolves.
- ❑ I will not take away my child's cell phone if he [or she] comes to me regarding inappropriate content received from someone else.

Child's Signature: _____ Today's Date: _____
Parent's Signature: _____ Today's Date: _____

In a scene from an episode of *Modern Family*, mom Claire is talking:

> Claire: "I'm feeling a little bit disconnected from Alex right now. Last week, I picked up her cell phone thinking it was mine and I accidentally read a few flirty text messages that were probably from a boy in her class, which is fine . . . or they're from a drifter."[10]

Later in the episode:

> Alex (*obviously having boy trouble*): "I'm never going back to school now."
> Claire (*in an attempt to help*): "No, sweetheart. Yes, you are. You are going back to school, but listen to me. Just because a boy sends you flirty texts doesn't mean you have to text him back."
> Alex (*outraged*): "What? YOU READ MY TEXTS?"
> Haley (*other daughter, walking in*): "YOU READ HER TEXTS?!"[11]

Oh, the outrage! What are we as parents to do? To read or not to read; that is the question.

Look over what a son and his father had to say about the topic of parents monitoring their child's media.

> About a year ago, my dad started monitoring my Facebook page. It's super annoying. He can see everything I write and everything my friends write. He watches everything. Do I mind him monitoring my Facebook page? Yes, I do.
> —14-year-old boy

> I wish my son would understand that anything he posts online is not private. Posted information is public, searchable and permanent. . . . As it turns out, my little boy, my little

angel, is not so angelic. Unfortunately, he had already learned the freedoms of social networking before I decided to take a look at what was going on.

—father of the 14-year-old boy[12]

And here's a take on the subject by a virtual dad:

Privileges (such as Facebook, driving, staying up late, etc.) are just that . . . privileges. As a minor, in my care, you have to demonstrate the responsibility that goes along with those privileges. I won't let you drive if I find that you've been drinking, and I won't let you use Facebook if I find that you've been using it inappropriately either.[13]

Can you identify with any of these parents? Can you understand the 14-year-old's point of view? Do you agree with any of them?

When we talk about setting digital boundaries, monitoring our kids' media, checking texts and following digital footprints, the topic of privacy eventually comes up. Do our kids need their privacy? Should parents respect their children's privacy? Do you have the right to invade your children's privacy? Do you have a responsibility to invade your children's privacy? Is it okay to spy on your kids? *Are* you spying on your kids?

All of those questions are questions I have been asked or have seen online surrounding the topic of our children and their privacy. While there is no specific verse or command that says, "Thou shalt not invade thy kid's privacy," there are guidelines and research that will help us as parents understand what our kids need and when they need it. As we raise our children from birth to adulthood, our parenting style moves from control to influence so that we can move our children from dependence to independence.

When our children are young, and because we are physically bigger than they are, we can get them to do something or stop them from doing something by physically steering them in the direction we want them to go. When you are in a store and you want your child to turn left, a gentle hand on the shoulder with a slight pull to the left corrects the course. (It was easier then, wasn't it?)

As our children get older, physical control diminishes and relational influence takes over. This relationship allows us to talk with them and include them in the decision-making process. Our children will also be more likely to share their lives with us if they have a good relationship with us. You've probably heard the phrase "Rules without relationship will lead to rebellion." While that statement is usually true, I would suggest the following phrase: "Rules with relationship will often lead to respect."

Now, I will tell you what we do when it comes to our kids' privacy. We do randomly check our kids' devices, and our kids know we check. Whether we are in the car, walking around, sitting in an airport or on vacation, we may simply turn to one of our kids and say, "Let me see your phone for a minute." It's random, unplanned and unscripted. We cycle through their texts, look at their pictures, and check their browser history. This process usually leads to a conversation and, no, it's not always bad. Most often it's a good conversation about a video they shot or a picture they took or what they posted. Occasionally, we have a difficult conversation, discuss boundaries or, sometimes, enforce a consequence. The important component is communication.

A red flag should go up if you ask to see your child's phone and all the texts have been erased, the browser history has been deleted and there are no pictures on the phone. From one parent to another, this most likely means your child is hiding something and doesn't want you to see.

Trust & Privacy Banking

At the bank of Craig and Mary, our children can make deposits, withdrawals, earn interest and manage their trust accounts on their own. But our children do not have total "banking" privacy. When the question comes up in our home about privacy, we check their trust account statements.

Do our children deserve privacy? Does the bank deserve to give you money? The answer to each question could be yes or could be no. If you have a zero balance in your bank account, then no, the bank does not deserve to give you money. The same is true in our home. Do our kids deserve privacy? It depends on how much trust money they have in their account. I do believe that as children get older, they should have some level of privacy for healthy personal growth. However, as a parent, I have a responsibility to teach and prepare my children for adulthood and to protect them while they are in cyberspace. I like what family psychologist Dr. Keith Kanner says when talking about privacy as it relates to the Internet:

> Teens need some privacy to feel independent and trusted by their parents. . . . [But the doctor also says that although] "supervision" is essential to protect children, . . . mental and physical privacy is also important. When parents interrogate or demand knowledge from their kids, like "no secrets," right away teens feel like they must have done something wrong and they are in trouble. Often, that means that the game is over right there. This type of overprotection can create a bad cycle.[14]

As a parent, it's often easier to be demanding rather than discerning. We are bigger and stronger and have all the power, so we feel as if we can demand and control much easier than set aside the time to explain things or take them out and talk about them. We may be able to accomplish quite a bit more if we were to take a moment to discern rather than a second to demand. (Just something to think about.)

Let's go old school for a moment. Let's say that when I was younger I wanted to go to the mall and walk around for a few hours. While at the mall, I may want to get into a car with a stranger or maybe take candy from someone I don't know. In any case, I want the option to do what I want. I may also want to hand out my address to a few people and tell them when I am home alone. Given this old-school example, what do you think a healthy parental response should be? How about, "No. You may not go unless I go with you."

Now back to the modern world. Let's say that when our children were younger they wanted to surf around the Internet for a few hours. While looking around, they decide to get into a digital car with someone they have never met, take some digital candy and exchange a few messages and pictures. They accept the person's friend request and give them a digital address as well. Given this example, what do you think a healthy parental response should be? How about, "No, you may not go unless I go with you."

Privacy and trust go together—one account linked to the other. If a child has earned his or her parents' trust, he or she buys more privacy. If the child's behavior causes the parents to doubt, the child makes a withdrawal and loses privacy until his or her trust account has been replenished.

While you may respect your children's privacy, let them know you intend to randomly monitor their activity. Be up-front about it. Mary and I tell our kids up-front that we will watch their digital footprint. They know that we will check their texts and emails. This is not something we do every day, but on random occasions.

The same goes for our children's rooms and backpacks. When we check their rooms or texts, and everything is good, they make a deposit in our parent trust bank. They can buy privacy and freedom with their trust balance. If we ask to see their phone and notice there isn't one text or email, meaning these have been erased, then they make a withdrawal from the parental trust account. When that happens, they go into debt and suffer its consequences.

I use the banking analogy because as adults it's easy for us to understand. A bank account is an in and out account. You put the money you earn into the account and you take money out of your account to pay bills and enjoy life. If you have a zero balance in your account, you can't buy anything. Occasionally, you may find your account overdrawn. The same is true for our children at the bank of trust and privacy.

A few of the areas we check with our children are their texts, pictures, social media accounts, browser history, emails, Xbox community and Netflix history. We don't tell our children when we will check or how often. When we check one or a few of the above-mentioned media, and all is well, that child makes a large deposit into the bank of trust and privacy. If we check browser history and it has been deleted, the child makes a withdrawal at the bank. Our kids earn our trust in other ways as well, not just online.

Here are five ways our children earn trust in our home:

1. Being truthful
2. Being where they should be
3. Being responsible
4. Being reachable
5. Being home on time

Checking your child's texts or monitoring your child's media is not spying; it's responsible parenting. Spying is an activity engaged in by someone who keeps a secret watch on the actions of others. Be very open about your intentions and why you are monitoring their media. I like what Ronald Reagan said: "Trust but verify." (Review chapter 7 and the "Rules for Maintaining a Healthy Social Media Account" in the Additional Resources for information on monitoring your child's use of social media.)

An Amendment to Think About

Amendment IV to our Constitution's Bill of Rights reads, "The right of the people to be secure in their persons, houses, papers, and effects, against unreasonable searches and seizures." I bring up the fourth amendment because of a workshop on at-risk youth that I once attended. One of the communicators at this workshop was a probation officer for teenagers. He told us a story that got everyone's attention, especially the attention of every parent in the room.

He explained that if your teenager breaks the law and is assigned a juvenile probation officer, your child becomes, as he put it, a "walking warrant." Wherever your child goes, he or she can be searched, as well as the location where that child is—all without a warrant. The teenager on probation *is* the warrant. In other words, if your teenager is assigned a parole officer for a crime he or she has committed, anything and everything in your house and grounds can be searched at any time of the day on any day of the year without notice. The point is, as a result of a child's behavior, his or her parents give up their right to the fourth amendment.

Now, you may be thinking, *My teenagers are good kids; they don't get into that kind of trouble.* Yes, I completely understand. I simply want you to understand that until our kids are 18 years old, not only are we responsible for teaching them right behavior, but also, according to the law, we are responsible for the consequences of their behavior. Now, with that in mind, wouldn't it be easier to look at your child's texts or check his or her room on occasion? Or would you like a police officer to do it for you?

9

Keep Communication Open

www.whowillyouempower.com/communicationopen

In high school, I took Latin. No, I don't know why. No one speaks Latin. It was harder than Spanish, and I don't remember anything that was taught except something about a pig. Anyway, one of the things I remember most is that if I didn't learn the vocabulary, I couldn't understand what was being said. So we were constantly being tested on vocabulary. It's a similar situation for parents. Kids are using a vocabulary you may not be aware of, and you simply cannot have a conversation with your child if you don't have the vocabulary.

Taking a page out of ABC's *Modern Family*, the socially unaware dad, Phil Dunphy, lets us know, "I'm the cool dad; that's my thang. I'm hip. I surf the Web. I text. LOL—Laugh Out Loud; OMG—Oh my gosh; WTF—Why the Face? And I know all the dances to *High School Musical*. (Kids sigh)"[1] Clearly, Phil does not understand the language. The question is, do you? Do I? Here's a quick texting quiz for you. Fill in the correct words after the abbreviated text. Answers are at the bottom.

How Is Your Digital Savvy?

- BTW
- LOL
- IDK
- WDYT
- IMHO
- TTYL
- B4N
- DIKU
- F2F
- PIR

Targeting Our Teens

We may have the language, we may know the vocabulary, but that doesn't mean we don't have to learn anything else. With new technology will come new responsibility as parents. One of the most important efforts we as parents can make is to keep communication open, and keep it open about uncomfortable topics. Our modern families are in an ancient battle being waged with modern weapons. Take a look at Ephesians 6:10-12:

> Be strong in the Lord and in his mighty power. Put on all of God's armor so that you will be able to stand firm against all strategies of the Devil. For we are not fighting against flesh-and-blood enemies, but against evil rulers and authorities of the unseen world, against mighty powers in this dark world, and against evil spirits in the heavenly places (Eph. 6:10-12).

Answers: By the way · Laugh out loud · I don't know · What do you think · In my humble opinion · Talk to you later · By for now · Do I know you · Face to face · Parents in room

Do you see the word "strategies"? It's a reference to how the devil operates. Without getting too deep, the Greek word used here is *methodeia*. Kind of looks like our English word "method." Have you ever heard the quote, "There is a method to their madness"? When used about someone, it means that, despite what it looks like, the person is extremely organized and purposeful in his or her actions. The person has skillfully and artfully planned and is ready to attack, not by rushing the target, but with tactical precision and cunning.

Personally, I think it's easier to encounter an enemy that's visible and rushing me than one that's behind the scenes, strategizing the best way to attack me. And that's it, isn't it? Our enemy has a plan, a series of maneuvers, a method to his madness. No, I'm not saying the Internet is evil; it's a content delivery system. But don't think for a minute that it can't be used as a tool in the hands of the enemy.

That Digital Tree in the Middle of the Room

I spoke to a marriage and family counselor who works primarily with teens. I asked him how many students he works with have either experienced or are experiencing the effects from Internet-related pornography. His response? "Craig, it's pervasive." My counselor friend is not alone in his thinking:

> Many parents' greatest fear concerning the Internet is that their children will encounter and be harmed by online pornography. These fears are well grounded. Research conducted over the past decade has documented significant rates of exposure for both boys and girls. One team of researchers concluded that "exposure to online pornography might have reached a point where it can be characterized as normative among youth Internet users, especially teenage boys."[2]

Remember the one thing God told Adam not to do in the Garden of Eden?

But the LORD told him, "You may eat fruit from any tree in the garden, except the one that has the power to let you know the difference between right and wrong. If you eat any fruit from that tree, you will die before the day is over!" (Gen. 2:16-17, CEV).

Remember what happened after Adam and Eve ate the fruit, and God came looking for them?

The man and woman heard the LORD God walking in the garden. They were frightened and hid behind some trees (Gen. 3:8, CEV).

Our children have been born into a digital garden with a million trees they have been told not to touch. They have been told to do their homework on it, study on it, use it for research and play a few games for enjoyment, but all around those activities are trees they are not supposed to touch. When (or if) our kids take the digital fruit from a tree they weren't supposed to touch, they will want to hide. Why? For the same reason you and I want to hide, for the same reason Adam and Eve wanted to hide: guilt, fear, failure, embarrassment, shame and regret.

The difference between our kids and the original occupants of the Garden is that our kids don't hide behind trees; they erase their digital footprints. Cleaning up a digital footprint by deleting browser history is a way to hide where you have been online. The garden today is different, but the feelings of failure, shame and regret are the same. In that moment when you find your child trying to hide something he or she did online, may I suggest remembering Ephesians 6:4: "Don't exasperate your children by coming down hard on them. Take them by the hand and lead them in the way of the Master" (THE MESSAGE).

The difficult thing about online pornography is that our kids may not even be looking for it. But just like the serpent in the

Garden, it will come looking for them. I know of one student who was first introduced to online pornography while sitting in science class at junior high school. The student sitting next to him pulled up a video on his phone and then turned the phone in his direction. It piqued his curiosity.

In our modern world, accessibility to the inappropriate is much easier and creates more consequences than when we weren't digitally connected. I like what the media mogul David Sarnoff said: "We are too prone to make technological instruments the scapegoats for the sins of those who wield them. The products of modern science are not in themselves good or bad; it is the way they are used that determines their value."[3]

Remember when God came looking for Adam and Eve? Genesis 3:9 records that God spoke three very important words: "Then the LORD God called to the man, 'Where are you?'" God wasn't asking for their location; He was asking what condition they were in. We need to look for our children in this way and look after them in their digital garden. Looking for them—looking for their condition and looking after them—requires keeping communication open.

Have you ever thought about what would have happened if God had not gone looking for Adam and Eve? I am going to assume they would have kept eating from the tree, realizing they were still ashamed, and later understanding that no one really cared. There would have been no need to hide. Why hide if nobody is looking? As parents, our children need to know that we are looking for them, not just watching them.

Five Digital Topics to Talk About with Your Teen

1. Cyberbullying
Cyberbullying is the use of any form of electronic media to tease, harass, threaten, embarrass, intimidate or humiliate another person online. The old-school definition of bullying included many of the

same words: "tease," "harass," "threaten" and "humiliate." The old-school definition also included the bully being present when the harassment was taking place. Usually, a bully was larger and stronger than other kids (think David and Goliath), just in case the bully had to back up his or her intimidating tactics. But new-school bullying—cyberbullying—is much different, and it's getting worse:

> Cyber Bullying is becoming more and more prevalent. From kids getting together on Facebook to "kick a ginger," to bullies posting videos of their attacks, we have a whole new world of brutality for kids to worry about.[4]

Anyone can be a victim of cyberbullying, but students are the most frequent targets. "From fake Facebook pages to the posting of embarrassing videos and photos, more than 20 percent of today's U.S. students age 10 to 18 report being a victim of cyber bullying."[5] Today's cyberbullies can hide behind a mask of obscurity while conducting attacks on their victims. Their obscurity often makes them harder to find. Some states no longer tolerate online harassment and have passed or are working on passing laws to arrest and prosecute cyberbullies.

Cyberbullying laws vary from state to state. One of the most stringent states in the country is Missouri:

> The suicide of a 13-year old girl who was the victim of an Internet hoax greatly raised the awareness of cyberbullying and its consequences in the state of Missouri. Governor Matt Blunt went so far as to create a task force whose sole purpose was to study and create laws regarding cyberbullying. As a result, the Internet Harassment Task Force now stands as a shining example for other states around the country. Missouri has also toughened their laws on the matter, upgrading cyber-harassment from a misdemeanor to a Class D felony.[6]

Cyberbullying may occasionally get passed off as a joke. Taking an embarrassing picture of someone and posting it, or writing a few funny remarks to someone or about someone, may not be illegal but could be inappropriate. Help your kids to be mindful of others' feelings. Scripture tells us, "Don't become like the people of this world. Instead, change the way you think. Then you will always be able to determine what God really wants—what is good, pleasing, and perfect" (Rom. 12:2, *GOD'S WORD*).

Here are three things you can do if your child has been cyberbullied:

1. *Record it.* Tell your child to record the bullying but not to retaliate. Take a screen shot of the computer screen (or cell-phone screen), and document the date and time and who the person is, if you know him or her.
2. *Report it.* If the bullying happened on a social media site, then let that site know what has happened and the content that was displayed. If the bullying is by phone, tell the cell phone company. If your child's peers at school are doing the bullying, report it to the school's administration. If the bullying includes a threat of violence, sexually explicit content, or stalking, then law enforcement officers need to be informed.
3. *Research it.* Know the cyberbullying laws in your state. Find out what the bullying prevention policy is in your child's school.

There are several websites that can give us insight and direction as parents. Here are a few that are worth exploring:

- *StopBullying.gov.* A site that explains what cyberbullying is, how to prevent it, how to report it, and what the laws are in each state. Currently, there are no federal laws that directly address cyberbullying.
- *Cyberbullyalert.com.* A software that assists you and your child in documenting threats you or your child have experienced while online.

• *Commonsensemedia.org/cyberbullying.* This site is filled with information and advice for parents and educators on cyberbullying, including how to teach children ages 2-17 about cyberbullying. The site also offers a free cyberbullying tool kit to help educators and schools.

2. Sexting

Sexting is sending, receiving or forwarding sexually explicit content, usually between mobile phones, and it may be happening more frequently than you think—with severe consequences.

The National Campaign to Prevent Teen and Unplanned Pregnancy and *CosmoGirl.com* found that 22 percent of girls ages 13-19, and 18 percent of boys ages 13-19 have sent or posted online nude or semi-nude images of themselves.[7]

When sending a sexually suggestive text without a picture, the number increases to 37 percent of girls and 40 percent of boys, with 48 percent of all teens between the ages of 13 and 19 saying they have received such a message.[8]

Most of the sexting between teens happens within the context of a boyfriend/girlfriend relationship, with girls sending most of the suggestive images to their boyfriends. The consequences of sexting are compounded when the relationship dissolves and the boyfriend forwards the picture to his friends in an attempt to humiliate or embarrass the girl. Let me give you just one example:

> [A high school girl] had sent nude pictures of herself to a boyfriend. When they broke up, he sent them to other high school girls. The girls were harassing her, calling her [names]. She was miserable and depressed, afraid even to go to school. . . .
>
> [She went on a] Cincinnati television station to tell her story. Her purpose was simple: "I just want to make sure no one else will have to go through this again."
>
> The interview was in May 2008. Two months later, [the teen] hanged herself in her bedroom. She was 18.[9]

This is not the only time that a teen has committed suicide because of sexting. There are also legal consequences for sexting. Like the laws for cyberbullying, each state has its own laws for sexting, which are usually the same laws that were set up to prosecute pedophiles and people who distribute pornographic content of minors. Teens in some states, like Florida and Pennsylvania, have been prosecuted or threatened with prosecution on child pornography laws because they sent out nude images through text messages. That's what happened to one Florida teen:

> He had just turned 18 when he sent a naked photo of his 16-year-old girlfriend, a photo she had taken and sent him, to dozens of her friends and family after an argument. . . .
> [The teen] was arrested and charged with sending child pornography, a felony to which he pleaded no contest but was later convicted. He was sentenced to five years probation and required by Florida law to register as a sex offender.[10]

One teen who was prosecuted as a sex offender said, "I made a small mistake but it turns out to be a big charge."[11]

Here are four things to do if you find inappropriate content on your child's cell phone:

1. *Respond; don't react.* When you come across a sext or text on your child's phone, the natural response will be to react. What I mean by react is freak out, yell, point, lecture, accuse and rant. I certainly understand. In some ways, it almost feels justifiable. Believe me, I have been there, yelled that. If you do find something inappropriate on your child's cell phone, create some space between you and your child to collect your thoughts. When you do this, you are not saying that what you saw or what you discovered was okay or that you condone the behavior. You simply don't want to allow your

emotions to dictate your response. "And now a word to you parents. Don't keep on scolding and nagging your children, making them angry and resentful. Rather, bring them up with the loving discipline the Lord himself approves, with suggestions and godly advice" (Eph. 6:4, *TLB*).

2. *Remember when.* Take a stroll down memory lane for a moment. Think back to your worst day as a teenager. What happened? Where were you? How did you feel? Did you get caught? What were the consequences? I ask those questions to give you a little perspective. I wonder if each of us would have acted the same today, given the power of social media and the Internet. I don't know about you, but I got in quite a bit of trouble without technology. I would have probably done more damage if I had had a powerful computer in my hand that could connect to the world from wherever I was at the time.

3. *Realize the opportunity.* If your primary reaction style of parenting is to hammer away, then your child may feel like a nail. How many parenting tools do you have in your belt? You can't build a house using only a hammer. Stringent rules without relationship may lead to further rebellion. Realize the opportunity to deepen your relationship with your child. "God's Spirit doesn't make cowards out of us. The Spirit gives us power, love, and self-control" (2 Tim. 1:7, *CEV*).

4. *Follow the plan.* If you are aware that sexting may occur, then having an appropriate consequence in place will make this next step easier. When you have a plan, the consequence feels more cause and effect than volatile reaction. I have, on occasion, overreacted when enforcing consequences for my kids' inappropriate behavior. For example, when one of my kids has been disrespectful, and I'm in a bad mood, I may say, "Okay, you are

grounded for a week! And give me your cell phone. You have lost all screen time and outside activities until Jesus comes back!" A slight overreaction? Yes. What I am saying is, be prepared. To whatever extent you can do it, know in advance the consequences for your child's behavior.

Having frequent and open conversations with your child about sexting is imperative in our modern families. The National Center for Missing and Exploited Children suggests discussing the following five points in order to prevent sexting.

Five Tips to Prevent Sexting

1. Think about the consequences of taking, sending, or forwarding a sexual picture of yourself or someone else underage. You could get kicked off of sports teams, face humiliation, lose educational opportunities and even get in trouble with the law.
2. Never take images of yourself that you wouldn't want everyone—your classmates, your teachers, your family or your employers—to see.
3. Before hitting send, remember that you cannot control where this image may travel. What you send to a boyfriend or girlfriend could easily end up with their friends, and their friends, and their friends.
4. If you forward a sexual picture of someone underage, you are as responsible for this image as the original sender. You could face child pornography charges, go to jail and have to register as a sex offender.
5. Report any nude pictures you receive on your cell phone to an adult you trust. Do not delete the message. Instead, get your parents or guardians, teachers and school counselors involved immediately.[12]

3. Posting

We live in a split-second world of send it now, worry about it later. The difference between responding and reacting is more important now than ever before. Once you post, it's no longer private; in fact, it could go viral. Even a direct message intended for one person on Twitter, or a private message on Facebook, or an email designed for one recipient can be copied, recorded and forwarded in a moment's notice. The consequences of such a post may not be felt within the first week or first year; but one day, when interviewing for a job, the question may come up, "So, tell me about this picture you sent a few years ago." Or, "Can you elaborate a bit on this video of you destroying public property before we get started with the interview?"

When I was a teenager, I wasn't exactly known for thinking things through. I can't speak for you, but some of our closest friends who are in our age bracket echoed the sentiment that there is a general theme of most teenagers not thinking things through, or of acting in the moment without thought of any future consequences. Prior to all things digital, impulsive behavior was usually contained by whoever was present to watch what happened or hear what happened at the time it happened. Our impetuous decisions as teenagers weren't documented to be viewed later by a future employer. Today, whatever our children post online may be recalled at a time when they don't want it to be. Once it's posted, it's public, simple as that.

As a teenager with undiagnosed ADD, I was frequently an "opportunity." I thought it would be cool to ride up to the local grocery store on my bike with a friend while my mom was at work. Why? To get that wonderful 70s invention, Pepsi Light! I loved it. I wanted it. I had the money for it. I went to get it. Actually, I left with my friend for the short ride with all 10 fingers and ended up in the hospital with 9! Why, you ask? Impulse control. (Why ride all the way to the store to get one Pepsi Light when you can get two?)

Riding home slowly on the sidewalk, holding two glass bottle beverages, isn't that fun, so why not do a few jumps off the curb?

The last curb I jumped is when I lost control of the bike. I ended up breaking both bottles, sliding on the street in the broken glass, cutting the entire right side of my body, and cutting off my finger. Later, in the hospital, the doctors reattached my finger, but the scar remains to this day.

I wish I could say this was the only example of a disastrous momentary impulse I had as a teenager, but that wouldn't be true. Breaking my arm in the same spot the day I got my cast off from the first break, getting my leg stuck on barbed wire, breaking the finger I cut off after I had the original cast removed . . . do you see the pattern? Maybe I wasn't the "typical" kid, but I think it's fair to say that most kids don't think before they act. Posting an image or text online would have given me the ability to make things worse at a much faster rate and have them permanently documented for all to see.

When talking to your children about posting to online social communities, give them five easy actions that will make it a S.M.A.R.T. post.

S*top*

If your emotions are running high and your thumbs are flying on the phone, stop.

"Don't use foul or abusive language. Let everything you say be good and helpful, so that your words will be an encouragement to those who hear them" (Eph. 4:29).

M*ove*

Move away for a moment. Put some time between you and the post so that your emotions are not running at peak capacity. "You must all be quick to listen, slow to speak, and slow to get angry" (Jas. 1:19).

A*djust*

Take a look at what you have written and make adjustments. "Wise people think before they act; fools don't—and even brag about their foolishness" (Prov. 13:16).

Review
Review what you have written with someone and get his or her feedback. "Plans go wrong for lack of advice; many advisers bring success" (Prov. 15:22).

Tell
If all is okay, tell it. "Everything you say should be kind and well thought out" (Col. 4:6, *GOD'S WORD*).

Remind your children that before they press send, they have to make sure it's smart!

4. Stealing
Discuss with your children that just because it's online doesn't mean it's free. That picture, song, story or book they are downloading may be someone's intellectual or creative property. You'll have to remind them that just because it's available online and easy to take doesn't make it legal or right to do so. Inform your kids that some sites or content creators let people use things they have produced for free as long as they get credit with an appropriate attribution. The content creator will usually let you know how and where to add that credit.

Have a further discussion with your kids about why people often consider Internet material as fair game. For example, you could say that when you take something online that isn't yours, it doesn't feel like stealing. Take a song for example. If you walk into a store that sells CDs and you see one you want, and you put it in your pocket and walk out without paying, you have stolen someone's property. Now, let's say you walk into a digital space and see that same CD. You click it, download it, and put it in your digital pocket without paying. You have stolen someone's property—the difference most likely being how you feel about the two events. It may feel like stealing when you remove physical property from a brick and mortar building, but it's easy to feel like you're borrowing when you take it from a digital space. Regardless of how you feel about taking something physically or taking something digitally, both are stealing. Help your kids to practice responsible behavior on the Internet.

5. Expectations

Have clear expectations about the use of all the electronic devices in your home and make sure your children understand those expectations. What do you consider to be appropriate or inappropriate use of the Xbox, computer, tablet or cell phone? How much time is too much time online? How old should your kids be before they get a cell phone?

One of the biggest challenges for families is how much time is too much time online and connected. We have talked about this in previous chapters, and this is largely a family-by-family conversation, but there are some statistics worth noting. According to a Kaiser Family Foundation study in 2009, on average, youth spend more than two hours daily talking and texting on cellphones, including 33 minutes talking and 95 minutes texting. Just over half of youth (56 percent) talk on a cell each day, spending nearly an hour in conversation. Slightly under half of youth (46 percent) text each day; but those who do text send an average of 118 texts per day.[13] (I don't give you these statistics to scare you, but to help you understand that our children are engaging the world in their own way.)

Some parents may have mixed feelings about all things digital. Some may have feelings of vulnerability because they don't understand the technology, or they understand the technology but don't like it. Other parents may have feelings of fear about the technology because they don't know how to parent in a world that is mostly digital. Still others may have feelings of worry about how their kids will do later in life. Will they be able to have a face-to-face conversation with someone? Will they be able to carry on an intelligent conversation in a job interview? Here's my answer: I don't know.

I can tell you that I understand all of those feelings. Mary and I have felt most, if not all, of the feelings I described—from vulnerability to fear to worry. Here are a couple of thoughts as we finish this section: Maybe when our kids go to a job interview, they won't have to talk. Maybe they won't even need to go to an interview. Maybe their résumé is on their fingernail, and when they shake hands with a potential employer the information downloads to his or her fingernail and uploads to a central database with the snap of a finger. From the cloud, the company's HR department can review and respond with a few questions that can be answered by recording a video and sending it back to the cloud where it can be forwarded to decision makers around the world.

If you ask me to give my gut feeling or prediction about the future, I would say that a child today who has the ability to interact and provide face-to-face customer service in an emotionally intelligent way will be the new rich tomorrow. I am also of the opinion that if your child does not know how to interact digitally, he or she will be the new poor, and I don't mean financially. They will miss out on community, creativity, information and all the amazing benefits the Net has to offer us.

I can't wait to see the possibilities technology will bring to us in the future. As I've already said, my mom always warned me to never get into a car with a stranger. That parenting advice is still good today. The only thing that has changed is the vehicle.

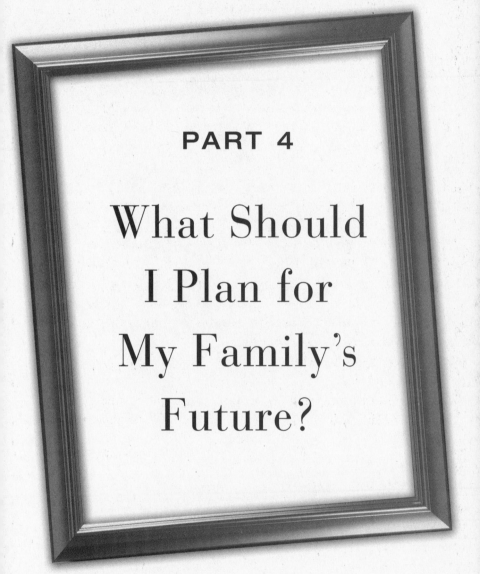

PART 4

What Should I Plan for My Family's Future?

10

Establish Your Family's Purpose

The only thing worse than being blind is having sight but no vision.
HELEN KELLER, AMERICAN AUTHOR AND ACTIVIST

Pick up any book on how to build a successful business and you will find a common thread running through all of them. That thread is made up of a vision for the future, a strategic mission statement to help you reach the vision, a set of guiding core values, and a few attainable goals. Each of these things is needed if you want to start, grow and flourish as a company.

Now, if you were to walk into a bank tomorrow and apply for a small business loan to get your company going, you would be asked to present your business plan. The bank would want to know what you plan to do with the loan, how you will be profitable should they give you the loan, and how you plan to repay the loan once you have been approved for the loan. A successful business is built on some very basic fundamentals. The same is true for our families.

I am convinced that if I had always approached my family with the same principles I approached work, I would have been more successful from the beginning. I don't know why I never applied the principles of starting a company to my family. It wasn't until I read *The Three Big Questions for a Frantic Family* by Patrick Lencioni that it clicked for me. What I read challenged me to think about vision, mission and values within the context of my family. Honestly, the concept felt a little cold and sterile to me; but the more time I allowed the idea to marinate in my heart, the more enthusiastic and convinced I became about this approach.

For years, I have been teaching others, through conferences and coaching, how to build a successful ministry or program. There is a process I walk all participants through to formulate a plan to move forward from where they are to where they want to be, and that doesn't happen by accident; it happens by being intentional and deliberate. A clear plan will focus your energy toward those things you want to become. Proverbs 17:24 reminds us that "an intelligent person aims at wise action, but a fool starts off in many directions" (*GNB*). If you have no plan, you have no direction.

Aiming at wise action means we must have a target to shoot at, a goal to reach. Whether we are starting Widget, Inc. or Family, Inc., we must have a purpose, priorities and a process. Otherwise, we may end up on an adventure much like Alice in Wonderland:

> "Would you tell me, please, which way I ought to go from here?"
>
> "That depends a good deal on where you want to get to," said the Cat.
>
> "I don't much care where—" said Alice.
>
> "Then it doesn't matter which way you go," said the Cat.[1]

For those parents who have older children in the home—age 13 and up—you may be thinking, *Well, it's a little late for all this talk about a plan and direction now. We have gone 12 years without that stuff. It doesn't make too much sense to start now!*

Conventional wisdom may say that you are right, but conventional wisdom isn't what we are after. Unconventional wisdom says that it is never too late to start! Look, I speak from experience. I would love to tell you that Mary and I had a family vision and mission statement in place before our children were born, but we didn't. In fact, we just wrote our family vision statement, mission statement and core values a year ago! If we can do it at a "late" date, so can you!

Start Where You Are

If you have been operating without a plan, there is already a family culture in place, and that culture, although unwritten and unspoken, is alive. If you don't believe me, try this experiment: Announce to your entire family that you are starting a new practice of eating breakfast together as a family at 7:00 A.M., which will occur right after a one-mile, get-awake run! Now, as awkward as that practice may sound, it would have been universally accepted if you had written it down and were practicing it together as a family ever since your children were seven. Your kids might even say, "It's the way we do things around here."

How about announcing to your family that every night, Monday through Friday, you are going to spend 15 minutes together as a family reading from a book that mom and dad have selected. Protests? Probably. Picketing? Possibly. There will be problems for sure unless you had been reading to your kids for 15 minutes every night since they were in the crib. I know this to be true, because that's what we did with our kids. The "complaint" we got was, "Can't you read longer than 15 minutes?" If you asked our kids about the practice, they would say, "It's the way we do things around here."

I give you the above two examples so that you can be prepared for some family feedback as you plan your family's future. In fact, if your kids are older, include them in the process! Your kids may be more willing to support what they help create.

I also want to encourage you to stick with your plan for Family, Inc. We didn't have all the building blocks defined and in place in one week. It took time. Think in short-term steps so you can accomplish long-term results.

In these final three chapters, I want to focus on your future—what things you can do right now that will have significant impact on who you become; what your family will look like in three months if you plan for your family's future. I promise that if you take the content of the next few pages to heart and work through the final process, your family will be healthier as a result.

In this chapter, we will talk about your family's purpose. Specifically, your family foundation made up of your family vision statement and family mission statement.

Set the Five Building Blocks in Place

You are now the CEO of your own company, Family, Inc. Congratulations! You are about to undertake one of the most difficult and most rewarding experiences of your life. As CEO, you are responsible for the plan, purpose, people, program, priorities, process and possessions of your company. Sound overwhelming? It can be, unless you think ahead. If you take some time to plan now, you will have a better chance of success in the future. As we begin, let's take a look at the five building blocks needed to build Family, Inc. They include (1) foundation, (2) vision, (3) strategic mission, (4) core values and (5) attainable goals. In this chapter, we will take a look at the first three building blocks: foundation, vision and mission.

Your Foundation

A foundation is something you build on and build from. A solid foundation is essential whether you are building a company, a corporation, a house or a home, so you need to explore what your foundation will be. Where you build is just as important, if not more important, than how you build.

Several years ago, our family was walking along a beach in Northern California. The waves were pretty strong and the water was very cold. Our boys were about two years old at the time. I had Alec on my shoulders. As we walked back to the car, "Down, Daddy, down, down, down" was the repetitive chant from my very verbal son. I knew he wanted to play with the water; yes, *with* it, not in it. I put him down and kept a close watch on him but instinctively knew what would happen given enough time.

The way a two-year-old plays with the water is unique. Have you ever been at the beach and watched a two-year-old tease the water? It looked like Alec was almost daring the waves to catch him, even begging the waves to touch his little legs. As a wave rolled in then started to recede, Alec chased the water like he was trying to catch it. The ocean pulled back quickly just barely keeping out of Alec's reach.

Then the ocean came back at Alec with more speed than he had to escape it. Once the ocean spit out another wave, his face showed concern, then panic, then fear, in that order. Apparently two-year-olds don't have the ability to judge the speed of things moving away from them or coming at them. After the initial splash of the wave on the beach, Alec started to move in what appeared to be slow motion. He took a few steps as the water slowly overtook him. He could feel the water rising up past his ankles, (concern), then above his knees (panic), and finally he lost his balance (fear).

Aside from not being able to judge the speed of things, Alec had not noticed that the foundation he was now on was different from where he had started. His teasing of the waves had begun as he stood on a huge rock. Teasing and laughing at the waves, he had been emboldened with an attitude that said, "You can't get me if you wanted to." Occasionally, a huge wave would hit the rock he was standing on and he would get a healthy dose of ocean spray, but he would laugh in its face. He felt safe standing on the rock. But when he began to chase the waves, he got off the rock and went onto the sand.

The rock was solid; the sand was not. The rock was stable; the sand was not. The rock was strong; the sand was not. As he lay face-down in the sand, maybe Alec believed the ocean had changed its approach, and that's why he ended up falling. But we know that's not what changed. What had changed was where he was standing.

While Alec was standing on the sand, the wave had been able to undermine his footing and had forced him to fall. It wasn't how he was standing, but where he was standing that made the difference. The ocean didn't need to literally knock him over; it just needed to loosen his foundation. The same is true for your family. If you want sure footing and stability, you must start with a strong foundation. So, the question is, where do you want to build?

It won't matter that you've built a great structure if you build it in the wrong place. Jesus told a story about the importance of a strong foundation, and He shed light on what it takes to make a firm foundation:

> Anyone who listens to my teaching and follows it is wise, like a person who builds a house on solid rock. Though the rain comes in torrents and the floodwaters rise and the winds beat against that house, it won't collapse because it is built on bedrock. But anyone who hears my teaching and doesn't obey it is foolish, like a person who builds a house on sand. When the rains and floods come and the winds beat against that house, it will collapse with a mighty crash (Matt. 7:24-27).

If we listen and obey God's teaching, then we are building on a strong foundation. If we listen to God's teaching but don't obey, then we are building on soft sand that shifts when difficulties come or a crisis hits. The Bible is pretty clear on what our foundation should be and where we need to build: "For no one can lay any foundation other than the one we already have—Jesus Christ" (1 Cor. 3:11). In chapter 12, we will start our building process by selecting the components that make up a solid foundation from which to build your family's future.

See Clearly

We have spent a lot of time with ophthalmologists over the last several years. Our son Cameron had an eye injury when he was three, resulting in many surgeries and even more eye appointments. Each eye appointment is focused around one primary objective, and that is to improve his vision. We have yet to go to an appointment where the doctor has said, "Okay, today let's talk about geometry or play a game of tic-tac-toe." Vision—clear, unobstructed vision—is the purpose for our appointment.

Each time Cameron sits in the doctor's chair, he is asked to focus on a picture or object off in the distance. To examine his eyes, the doctor tries different lenses and makes small prescription corrections— all in an attempt to help him see what's in front of him more clearly.

I bring this story to your attention as a reminder that we all have a story about the state of our "vision." Some of us were raised in a loving and nurturing environment where there was much care, concern and compassion for our well-being. If you were loved and valued, today, as a parent, you see clearly. You can model for your children what your parents modeled so well for you.

There are some of us who have been injured as young children. My son's injury was a physical accident; but there are many of us whose parents may have been the cause of our injuries while growing up. Perhaps emotional and physical abuse was your normal. Maybe it was neglect or lack of concern for your well-being. Those early injuries affect the vision you have for your family. Even now, as an adult, you may think you were an accident if your parents uttered those words while you were growing up. I want to tell you right now that this is untrue. You *were* planned. God planned you for a purpose.

I want you to know that the parent you have been up to this point may be due to an injury you sustained many years ago, and it may be clouding your vision. Don't beat yourself up. The parent you are today is not the parent you can be tomorrow. Talking with a close friend or a wise counselor can help you clear your vision both as a person and as a parent. Sometimes a person must look back through a cloudy past in order to look forward to a clear future.

See the Future

Not only is vision about seeing clearly, but also it is about seeing the future. When we have a clear picture in our mind of what we want our family to become, our vision is ready. As discussed earlier, an emotional injury in your childhood may cloud your view of the future. God has amazing things waiting for you and your family; but if you can't see them, it is doubtful you will reach them. If your clarity of vision has fallen out of focus due to things in your past, then let's try on a few corrective lenses to see if we can't improve your vision.

When we take our son to the eye doctor, one of the first tests is for him to look at a distant object through what appears to be a huge pair of glasses; it's called a phoropter. You probably know the test from when the doctor repeated words like, "Which one of these is best? A or B? 1 or 2? Do you like it better like this, or like this?" Now, let's take our own vision test by looking at something in the distance, like our family, through a spiritual phoropter, to see if our vision improves.

- First Lens: *See*
  "Now stand here and see the great thing the Lord is about to do" (1 Sam. 12:16).
- Second Lens: *With*
  "Do not be afraid or discouraged, for the Lord will personally go ahead of you. He will be with you; he will neither fail you nor abandon you" (Deut. 31:8).
- Third Lens: *Courage*
  "So be strong and courageous! Do not be afraid and do not panic before them. For the Lord your God will personally go ahead of you. He will neither fail you nor abandon you" (Deut. 31:6).

- Fourth Lens: *Peace*
  "I am leaving you with a gift—peace of mind and heart. And the peace I give is a gift the world cannot give. So don't be troubled or afraid" (John 14:27).
- Fifth Lens: *Joy*
  "I pray that God, the source of hope, will fill you completely with joy and peace because you trust in him. Then you will overflow with confident hope through the power of the Holy Spirit" (Rom. 15:13).
- Sixth Lens: *Hope*
  "'For I know the plans I have for you,' says the Lord. 'They are plans for good and not for disaster, to give you a future and a hope'" (Jer. 29:11).
- Seventh Lens: *Continually*
  "Study this Book of Instruction continually. Meditate on it day and night so you will be sure to obey everything written in it. Only then will you prosper and succeed in all you do" (Josh. 1:8).

My hope is that these seven lenses will bring some clarity for you about your family's future. In fact, put all seven words together in a sentence as a powerful reminder:

See, with courage, peace, joy, hope, continually.

As our visual clarity improves, we can see things not as they are but as how we want them to be, and that's exactly what we want for our family's vision statement.

Your Vision

Your family vision statement is a short inspirational phrase that describes who you want your family to become, not who you are now. Let me say that again. Your vision statement is a phrase that describes who you want your family to become, not who you are now. It's your best picture of your family in the future. Here are a few examples of a family vision statement:

"Love God, Love Others."
"We Make a Difference Together!"
"Never Give Up."
"We Laugh, We Cry, We Always Try."

Before you laugh at the statement that rhymes, take a look at the final words of Apple Computers' vision statement in 1980: "Making tools for the mind that advance humankind."[2] (Who likes rhyming now?)

You may look at the last example and think, *We laugh and cry? What's up with that? I thought you said this is supposed to be the best picture of our family, the family we want to become; we want to be a family that doesn't cry.* I understand. But remember, each vision statement is unique to the family writing it. This statement may be a great vision for a family that rarely shares their feelings and has been disconnected for years. What they are saying is, We are going to feel more as a family. We are going to laugh more; we are going to cry and show emotion instead of stuffing it like we have done in the past. We are going to put effort into everything we do by trying new things, taking healthy risks and applying some faith as we move forward in our family. So, "We Laugh, We Cry, We Always Try!" Do you see how that statement can make a difference in one family's life?

Remember, this is your vision statement of what you want your family to become, not who you are now. I say that because I don't want you to get trapped into thinking you can't change or it's too late to change. I don't want anyone who has experienced an emotional injury growing up to think he or she doesn't deserve to be a good parent, can't be a good parent or is not capable of being a good parent. You are! Take a look back at who you are building your foundation on (if necessary, look again at 1 Cor. 3:11), and then read Matthew 19:26 out loud: "Jesus looked at them intently and said, 'Humanly speaking, it is impossible. But with God everything is possible.'" Yes, with God, everything is possible.

Let me hit the drum one more time. Your family vision statement will remind you of what you want your family to look like in the future, not who you are now. What kind of vision statement would this be: "We are stuck in a rut and fail at life, constantly argue and enjoy the strife"? Do you see where I am going with this? Who do you want your family to *become*? What do you aspire your family to be? What is your dream for your family?

Family Portrait

The final *Modern Family* episode of season one was about trying to get a family portrait taken. Throughout the show, we see the mom, Claire, planning and strategizing how to get everyone together for this one moment to capture their family life on film. Claire's vision for this portrait was for the entire family to be standing together, dressed in matching white outfits, smiling beautifully. And of course, it didn't go according to plan.

Most of the family didn't want to be there for the picture, and a series of mishaps just about derailed the shot altogether: a blemish on one, an argument from another, an accusation from a third, and things started to spiral out of control. Then Claire took command of the chaos:

> Claire: "We are going to get together and act like a normal family for one-tenth of a freaking second, and we're going to do it right now!"
> Jay (*Claire's dad chimes in*): "This is ridiculous ... you would be a lot happier if you weren't obsessed about everything being perfect. News flash, life is not perfect, Claire."[3]

How does anybody act like a normal family? What is normal? I say forget normal; think healthy. Claire bore the brunt of the negative comments, but the reality is that she was the one who had the vision of getting the family together for a portrait, and she held on to it. The vision was jeopardized when the mud started flying—literally.

Jay reached down, grabbed a handful of mud and smeared it on Claire's shirt. That started a chain reaction of mud smearing on every member of the extended family. Then, all dressed in mud-stained white clothes, the picture was taken.

Claire accomplished the vision she had set for her family, and a portrait of a happy, smiling, albeit muddy people could finally be hung in the entryway of their home. Your vision will be accomplished as well, but you should understand that life is messy, dirty and tough. Don't let those things get in the way of your family's vision. You may get a little dirty on your journey, but in the end, you will have a portrait of your family to be proud of—an exact likeness of the character, uniqueness and personality that *is* your family.

Your Mission

Before we look at what a mission statement can do for your family, let's look at what it does for a corporation. Specifically, why do successful corporations have a well-thought-out mission statement? Why is it so important? There are five reasons why corporations have a mission statement.

1. A mission statement explains why the corporation exists.
2. A mission statement changes the corporation's behavior.
3. A mission statement provides unity among corporation staff.
4. A mission statement fuels corporate decisions.
5. A mission statement focuses the corporation's future.

What if you took those same five reasons why corporations have a well-defined mission statement and applied them to your family? Would they really help your family members change their behavior? Would they fuel your decisions and explain why you exist? Could a well-defined mission statement increase the chances of Family, Inc.'s success? Yes, yes, yes and . . . yes!

1. A mission statement explains why your family exists.
2. A mission statement changes your family's behavior.
3. A mission statement provides unity among family members.
4. A mission statement fuels your family's decisions.
5. A mission statement focuses your family's future.

Now, you may be thinking, *What's the difference between vision and mission?*

A vision statement describes your family in the future. It's a picture of who you want to become. A mission statement gives you a set of instructions to reach your vision and, more importantly, it tells you why you are doing what you are doing. Your mission statement will describe why your family exists; it tells you why you live your life the way you do!

Describing your family's mission statement goes hand in hand with your family's vision statement. If your vision describes what you want your family to become, then your mission is the instruction booklet to accomplish your vision.

Vision and mission statements require effort and show intentionality. Are you being intentional with your family or are you leaving life up to chance? Are you acting thoughtlessly, or do you "understand what the Lord wants you to do" (Eph. 5:17)? We've already explored the importance of building a home on the right foundation. We have also seen the value of having a picture of what we want to build. But unless we have a clear set of plans that direct us how to build, we will never realize our vision.

When our boys where younger, the toys we bought them for their birthday or Christmas usually had a statement on the box that went something like this: "Some assembly required." As a new dad, I was somewhat baffled by the term "some" after I opened my first box. Apparently, there are different interpretations to the word. My advice to new dads is first, "Let the store put it together! It's worth the cost." Second, the word "some" usually, if not always, means "most." If you have twins, never ever leave the store without whatever it is you are buying fully assembled and operational.

The first few times I went to put a bike or toy together, I would discard the instructions and tip up the box. (Dads know where I am going with this.) The reason we tip up the box is to see the picture of what we are trying to build. We like to go by sight, not instructions. How hard can it be to put a toy together? As it turns out, the instructions are a key component to building the toy correctly. (Who knew?) The instructions give some valuable information, like what tools to use, a description of all the parts and the order in which you should build. When I would sit down to build the toys for my boys without the instructions, two things would inevitably occur. One, I would end up with extra parts, or worse, not enough parts! Two, I would end up disassembling a portion of the project because I missed a step, skipped a step or didn't even know there was a step. Looking at a picture is no substitute for reading the instructions. That's where our family mission statement comes in.

We can't simply look at the picture of who we want to become and start to build. We will end up having extra parts or undoing and redoing several steps, and never end up having it look like the picture. A set of instructions is the only way to build a solid home and a healthy family.

Determine Your Family's Priorities

*The key is not to prioritize what's on your schedule,
but to schedule your priorities.*
STEVEN COVEY, *THE SEVEN HABITS OF
HIGHLY EFFECTIVE PEOPLE*

Where our foundation, vision statement and mission statement help us with our purpose, our values and goals help us with our priorities. The use of the term "priorities" implies things that are in order of importance. We prioritize our to-do lists, our daily tasks and our time; but how do we know if our priorities are correct? What guidelines do we have in place that validate our priorities? How do we know what to shuffle to the top when we have a limited amount of time? The answer is values.

Values

Our values help us to prioritize everything in our life so that the important things get most of our time and effort and the least-important things get the least amount of our time and effort. When we take the time to define a core set of values for our family, prioritizing what happens in our family life becomes much easier and more focused.

For my seventh birthday, my mom took me and a few friends bowling. What I remember most about that party was how we bowled. I'm not talking about the score or the skill, both of which my friends and I didn't have much of. Let's just say we bowled in an unconventional way. When we arrived at the bowling alley, we checked in, got our shoes, chose a ball and headed to our lane. What we saw next was an answer to prayer. The people at the bowling alley had put these long bumper blockers in the gutters of the lane. Can you picture it?

There were eight seven-year-old kids standing in front of the lane with absolutely no chance of throwing a gutter ball. Every ball we threw down the lane that day hit something. In fact, later in the day, when "traditional" bowling was no longer working for us, we tried to see how many times we could bounce the ball off the bumpers before they hit the pins. Now, think of your family values like those bumpers. They prevent you from throwing gutter balls down the lane of life.

When you are writing your family values, the more specific and clear you make them, the more dynamic and helpful they become. "When your values are clear, making decisions becomes easier."[1] There are three reasons why clear values make decisions easier.

1. Clear Values Remove Doubt from Your Decisions

You don't have any doubts about your decision making because your values clarify things for you. "A person who has doubts shouldn't expect to receive anything from the Lord. A person who has doubts is thinking about two different things at the same time and can't make up his mind about anything" (Jas. 1:7-8, *GNB*).

2. Clear Values Remove Passion from the Process

Many times your values will make the right decision for you, despite what you are feeling at the time. Values don't have feelings. That doesn't make them insensitive, but it does make them unbiased. When your feelings want to hijack your family decisions, values come to the rescue and say yes or no without hesitation or reservation. Values remove extreme emotions from your decision-making process. They put bumpers in the gutters of your life decisions and keep you focused on how you are to proceed.

3. Clear Values Remove Opinion from the Outcome

Values don't ask for your opinion, they give it to you. You don't want to come up with your core values on a whim. You will want to take your time and make sure the values you define for your family are healthy and truthful. The time you have invested in defining your core family values will pay off in the long run when a tough decision is looming and you are having a difficult time removing your opinion from your decision. A well-written value will help you remove opinion so that you can achieve your outcome.

Tom Landry was the beloved coach of the Dallas Cowboys for 29 years. As a kid, I remember watching Landry coach on the sidelines. What amazed me and still sticks with me today was Landry's calm behavior no matter what the situation. No shouting, yelling or running up and down the sidelines. If his team kicked a field goal to win a playoff game in overtime, he remained calm, cool and collected. If a wrong call in the remaining seconds of a game caused his team to lose, he remained calm, cool and collected.

A reporter once asked him how he was able to maintain such a calm focus with all of the pressures. Coach Landry replied, "It's easy because I have my priorities straight. First is my God, second my wife, third my family and fourth is football; so if I [lose] on the weekend, I have lots of more important things to support me through the week."[2] Landry's priorities were in order because his values were clear. He was later quoted as saying, "Setting a goal is not the main thing. It is deciding how you will go about achieving it and staying with that plan."[3]

Our values act as guides for our behavior and help us decide how we go about accomplishing and achieving our plan. When we define our core values, in a very real sense, we are defining how we behave. The process works like this: Our core values provide a basis for our beliefs. Our beliefs fuel our behavior. Our behavior is what people around us observe. When you repeat a behavior long enough, it becomes a habit.

If you have never written down values for your family to live by, then can you imagine how your family life is about to change, for the better, over the next few months? Now, before we talk about goals, let's take a quick look at the seven ways our values help us.

1. Values Help Us Clarify Our Choices

Our values act as a filter to clarify our choices. How do we set the right goals for our family or make the best choice when presented with several options? We look through our values to bring things into focus. Are you being asked to get involved with something you really want to do but don't have time for? Look through your values to see if they bring clarity to your choices.

2. Values Help Us Select a Solution

Solutions can be a dime a dozen, but choosing the right solution for our family offers fewer options. Values help us select a solution by narrowing our options. There may be a time when you need to make a decision and you are presented with five good options. Each option is a really good option, but a well-written set of values can help you select a solution that's the best for your family.

3. Values Help Us Eliminate Our Emotions

I am not advocating that we eliminate our emotions altogether, just that they can get in the way of healthy decisions. Think of a time when your emotions were running high. Did those emotions help or hinder you from making the best decision possible? Passion and strong emotions can fuel a competitor's performance, but when emotions run high or out of control, they have the ability to make smart people stupid. Our values help us eliminate emotions from a decision-making process.

4. Values Help Us Guide Our Goals

Every goal we set should be processed through the lens of our values. When this occurs, we write our goals aligned with our values.

If we were to write a goal without guidance from our values, we might accomplish our vision but at what price? In this case, our values help us make our journey just as pleasant as the destination by guiding us gracefully toward our goals.

5. Values Help Us Determine Our Decisions

We make hundreds of decisions a day, from what we will eat to what we will read to what route we will drive to work. Most of those decisions happen naturally without really thinking about them. However, larger decisions take more time and pack more punch, so we must be more careful when determining those decisions. Clear values not only help us make tough decisions, but they will also help us be more consistent in making them.

6. Values Help Us Influence Our Impact

Not only do our values help us determine our decisions, but they also influence our impact by causing us to focus on what's most important. If we can move from being a "Jack of all trades" to a "master of one," our impact will be more focused and less dispersed. A list of well-written and focused values can help us influence our impact in the season in which we are living.

7. Values Help Us Focus Our Future

One of the biggest ways our values can help us achieve our goals and move us toward our vision is focus. Focus is different from clarity in one regard: Clarity will help us see all things accurately, whereas focus will help us concentrate on one thing among many clear ones.

For many of us, writing down our values and practicing them will mean breaking a few bad habits before instilling the new ones. So here are some straightforward and encouraging words from Galatians 6:9: "So let's not get tired of doing what is good. At just the right time we will reap a harvest of blessing if we don't give up."

Goals

Simply put, goals promote progress. We define our goals to help us move closer to our vision. They are the steps we take to act out our priorities and keep us diligently focused on our family's future. Each goal is a small step to big impact. Goals give us the awareness to invest our time and resources in the things that really make a difference in our family. They remind us of what we are working to achieve. Our goals should be explainable, attainable, observable, measurable and adaptable. Each of these components enables us to write goals that promote progress and empower change in our family (note the emphasis on "able" below). Now, let's take a quick look at five attributes of a well-written goal.

1. Goals Must Be ExplainABLE

The more specific your goals are, the more powerful they become. You may want to write a goal that speaks to the cleanliness of your kids' rooms. For example, "Each child will have his or her room clean by Sunday evening every week." Is this a good goal? If you like cleanliness and organization, then yes, it's a good goal. However, can we state anything to make it better? How about being more specific? I know that each of our three children would define "clean" three different ways; so why not create a specific reference point for what clean really means. Here's how we wrote the goal to make it more specific: "Each child will have their room *hotel*-clean by Sunday evening every week." Our kids have been in enough hotels to understand the language "hotel-clean"; so by adding one word, we changed the dynamic and power of the goal.

2. Goals Must Be AttainABLE

Goals must be reasonable and able to be accomplished. Write your goals so that they make you work to accomplish them; but don't make them so hard that you get frustrated and give up trying to reach them. On the other hand, if we consistently write goals that require little to no effort to accomplish, we will never stretch or change our behavior enough to really matter. Take Sam Walton for example. He set a goal for "my little Newport store to be the best, most profitable variety store in Arkansas within five years."[4] As you know, he went on to accomplish that goal, and he didn't stop there. He kept revising his goals to make Walmart one of the most successful stores in history. A statement that is often attributed to Walton reminds us that "A good goal should scare you a little and excite you a lot." When writing your family goals, aim high, miss low.

3. Goals Must Be ObservABLE

Can you observe the goals being accomplished or attempting to be accomplished? If you can see what is happening, then the goals are observable. If your goals are not observable, they're not measurable.

4. Goals Must Be MeasurABLE

You need to be able to see how much your goals are being met. Here are a few questions to consider: Are your goals all-or-nothing goals, or can they be tracked over time? Can you track the progress of your goal? Can you see how much of each of your goals is being accomplished, and what percent? Let's look at the room-cleaning goal again: "Each child will have his or her room hotel-clean by Sunday evening every week." This is a goal that is measurable. Let's say there are four children in your family, and over the last five weeks, three of your children have accomplished this goal. While three have accomplished it, your goal has not been fully met. Since your goal is measurable, you know you have 75 percent of your goal met. Now you can move on to the next step to see if you need to revise and adapt this particular goal.

5. Goals Must Be AdaptABLE

Make sure your goals can be revised or changed as time goes on. You want goals that have a little flexibility to them so that you can revise them if they aren't specific enough or if they are unclear. You also want to adapt a goal if it continues to be unattainable after repeated effort. Remember, our goals should help us achieve our vision, not work in the opposite direction by discouraging us to the point we want to give up trying.

• • •

Although writing goals according to each of the previous five steps may be easy, accomplishing them may be difficult. You need persistence to see them through. Proverbs says that the "plans of the persistent surely lead to productivity, but all who are hasty will surely become poor" (Prov. 21:5, *ISV*). Having an attitude of determination, courage and resilience is a key component when you feel like throwing in the towel. Be persistent and you will be productive with your goals.

12

Design Your Family's Process

An intelligent person aims at wise action,
but a fool starts off in many directions.
PROVERBS 17:24, *GNB*

Let's take a moment and remind ourselves of what we just learned. We learned that our foundation, vision statement and mission statement help us with our purpose; and we learned that our values and goals help us with our priorities. In this final chapter, we are going to bring it all together in a five-step process designed to plan your family's future!

The process is simple, but it will take some time to finish. Enjoy the process and set a reasonable pace to walk through each step. You don't need to rush the process, but don't let it drag either. The longer you wait between steps, the more momentum you lose. I echo the apostle Paul's words: "God is the one who began this good work in you, and I am certain that he won't stop before it is complete" (Phil. 1:6, *CEV*). If you get stuck, hang in there! Do something creative or different, or sit quietly and wait for God to speak.

Think of this chapter as a step-by-step guide to walk your family through the process of creating your Family, Inc.! There will be questions to answer, activities to complete and thoughts to record. You will brainstorm ideas and think creatively about the focus of your family. You can write your thoughts and ideas in the margin of your book if it's paper, or type them if it's digital. You can also download a workbook that will walk you through each of the five steps (see the link below). I recommend this option so that you can see the big picture as you work through each step. Again, the important thing is to keep moving through all five steps. Don't stop!

1. *Download the workbook.* If you choose to use the *Family, Inc.* workbook, you can download it at www.whowill youempower.com/familyinc.
2. *Be prepared.* Keep pen and paper or the workbook with you until you have completed all five steps. Be prepared to capture a word, thought, phrase or idea at any time.
3. *Invest the time.* Plan to spend 57 minutes on each step. It's probably more time than you need, but the extra time will bring you some balance.
4. *Take the steps.* Take each step in order starting with your foundation and finishing with your goals. Each step builds upon the next. Keep in mind the five building blocks we discussed in chapter 10.

Step 1: Deciding My Family's Foundation

Verse to Remember
"For no one can lay any foundation other than the one we already have—Jesus Christ" (1 Cor. 3:11).

Thoughts to Consider

Take a look at the following verses and inspirational quotes. Each one could serve as a foundation on which to build your family. Think about one of these being your family theme, your family verse or your family quote. It will be your family's foundation on which you will build your family's future.

Verses to consider:

1. "Serve one another" (Gal. 5:13).
2. "Let us think of ways to motivate one another to acts of love and good works" (Heb. 10:24).
3. "Put on your new nature, and be renewed as you learn to know your Creator and become like him" (Col. 3:10).
4. "I am writing to remind you, dear friends, that we should love one another. This is not a new commandment, but one we have had from the beginning" (2 John 1:5).
5. "Imitate God, therefore, in everything you do, because you are his dear children. Live a life filled with love, following the example of Christ. He loved us and offered himself as a sacrifice for us, a pleasing aroma to God" (Eph. 5:1).
6. "Therefore, accept each other just as Christ has accepted you so that God will be given glory" (Rom. 15:7).
7. "Supplement your faith with a generous provision of moral excellence, and moral excellence with knowledge, and knowledge with self-control, and self-control with patient endurance, and patient endurance with godliness, and godliness with brotherly affection, and brotherly affection with love for everyone" (2 Pet. 1:5-7).
8. "Be kind to each other, tenderhearted, forgiving one another, just as God through Christ has forgiven you" (Eph. 4:32).
9. "And whatever you do or say, do it as a representative of the Lord Jesus, giving thanks through him to God the Father" (Col. 3:17).

Inspirational Quotes to Consider

- "All greatness is achieved while performing outside your comfort zone." —Greg Arnold
- "Keep your face to the sunshine and you cannot see the shadows." —Helen Keller
- "The only people you should try and get even with are the ones who have helped you." —John E. Southard
- "Our life is what our thoughts make it." —Marcus Aurelius
- "It is better to deserve honors and not have them than to have them and not deserve them." —Mark Twain
- "It's not the mountain we conquer, but ourselves." —Sir Edmund Hillary
- "The difference between the possible and the impossible lies in a man's determination." —Tommy Lasorda
- "We are what we repeatedly do. Excellence, then, is not an act, but a habit." —Aristotle
- "Never stop growing. Plateaus should only be found in geography books, not in personal experiences." —John Maxwell

Actions to Take

Read through the verses and quotes a few times. Find one that catches your attention and resonates with your soul; one that you feel would best describe the type of foundation you want to build your family on. Once you select a verse or a quote you want as your foundation, then you are ready to move on to the next step.

I'm sure some families will go a little further when deciding their family's foundation. In fact, I hope you do! However, I don't want anyone to get stuck. I've provided some choices just to make the process enjoyable. Some families will use the verses or quotes provided as a springboard to explore other Bible verses or inspirational quote options. I say, explore, unleash and get creative!

Perhaps you don't need to start from scratch. Some families already have a foundation and may be doing a family renovation.

They just need to build a vision and mission addition and maybe do a remodel on their values and goals.

No matter where you are in regard to Family, Inc., before moving on to the next step, make sure you do the following three things:

1. You understand the importance of a firm foundation.
2. You have made a decision on your foundation.
3. You have written down your foundation verse or inspirational quote.

What We Have Accomplished

Foundation
So that you can see an example for each step in the design process, we are going to choose Colossians 3:17 as our sample family foundation:

Whatever you do or say, do it as a representative of the Lord Jesus, giving thanks through him to God the Father (Col. 3:17).

Step 2: Designing My Family's Vision

Verse to Remember
"Write the vision. Make it clear on tablets so that anyone can read it quickly" (Hab. 2:2, *GOD'S WORD*).

Thoughts to Consider
In this step, we are casting a vision of who you want your family to become, not who you are now. Think forward with hope, not back with regret. Think the way Paul thought when he said, "My friends, I don't feel that I have already arrived. But I forget what is behind, and I struggle for what is ahead" (Phil. 3:13, *CEV*).

Fulfilling the vision you have for your family is a never-ending pursuit. You won't accomplish it next week, next month or next year. Habakkuk 2:2-3 says,

> Write the vision. Make it clear on tablets so that anyone can read it quickly. The vision will still happen at the appointed time. It hurries toward its goal. It won't be a lie. If it's delayed, wait for it. It will certainly happen. It won't be late (*GOD'S WORD*).

This verse in Habakkuk tells us three things. First, make your vision clear. Second, write it down (he suggests tablets, but paper will work). Third, your vision will be accomplished over time. Once your vision statement is designed, you will spend the rest of your family life accomplishing it.

Actions to Take

In order to write our vision statement, we need a few good words. To get our minds going in the right direction, answer the following two questions. I have given you a few words as examples to get you started.

Question Number One:
What words or short phrases best describe the kind of family you want to become?

1. Kind hearted	8.	15.
2. Compassionate	9.	16.
3. Honest	10.	17.
4. Encouraging	11.	18.
5. Excellent	12.	19.
6.	13.	20.
7.	14.	21.

Question Number Two:
What things could you do to be a better family in the future?

1. Pray together	8.	15.
2. Go to church	9.	16.
3. Take vacations	10.	17.
4. Laugh together	11.	18.
5. Serve others	12.	19.
6.	13.	20.
7.	14.	21.

Select Five Answers
Once you have answered both questions, select five of your answers and write them down. The goal is to select a few words that will paint the best picture of who you want your family to become. Write those words below; then select a few you can mold into a short, personal statement you can remember! Here is an example:

1. *Compassionate*
2. *Serve others*
3. *Excellent in all things*
4. Encouraging
5. Pray together

Write Your Vision Statement
Based on the choices above, our sample Family, Inc. will have the following vision statement:

We are a family who does our absolute best for God and others.

Look at the actions you took, and you will see that the sample vision statement connects them.

1. We answered both questions.
2. We selected five words from the answers to the questions and then narrowed the list of words to three (the ones in italics).
3. We wrote our vision statement from the words we selected.

Here are examples of other vision statements:

- We are a family who serves others daily.
- We are a family who makes a difference in the world.
- We are a family who plays, prays and stays together.
- We are a family who practices grace, mercy and love.
- We are a family with transparent hearts practicing authentic behavior.

Remember that your vision statement won't tell you why your family exists, but it will tell you who you want to become. As you're thinking, discussing and writing, keep in mind three things:

- *Keep it memorable.* You can't become what you won't remember.
- *Keep it short.* Use no more than 140 characters. Make it tweetable!
- *Keep it personal.* This is about your family. Preserve your uniqueness!

What We Have Accomplished

We will carry what we have accomplished from previous steps through the remaining steps, so you can see how the process unfolds and our plan develops.

Foundation

"Whatever you do or say, do it as a representative of the Lord Jesus, giving thanks through him to God the Father" (Col. 3:17).

Vision
We are a family who does our absolute best for God and others.

Step 3: Describing My Family's Mission

Verse to Remember
"Don't act thoughtlessly, but understand what the Lord wants you to do" (Eph. 5:17).

Thoughts to Consider
Now here is some great news. By writing a mission statement for your family, you will eliminate just about every obstacle in the way of your family becoming what it was meant to be! If you have ever thought or said, "my work all seems so useless! I have spent my strength for nothing and to no purpose" (Isa. 49:4), then be prepared for a life change! After completing this step, you will have a purpose and direction for your family to follow, and you will know why your family has been placed in this world!

Let me tell you right up front that there is no one right way to write your family's mission statement. I wish there were a single rule to follow that would make writing your mission statement both simple and accurate. If you have never written a mission statement before, you may feel a little out of your element and already have more than a few questions. But the process you are about to follow will give you an ordered structure to follow, and you will be able to write a compelling mission statement for your family.

Actions to Take
Using the vision statement that we just wrote in step 2 ("We are a family who does our absolute best for God and others"), we are going to describe why our family exists in this world and why we live life the way we do. Our mission statement will give us a few

instructions, but the real power of the mission statement is that it tells us and reminds us why our family is here.

Think in terms of threes. For example, think of "Life, liberty and the pursuit of happiness"—three rights written by Thomas Jefferson when he wrote the Declaration of Independence. Jefferson was a gifted writer and communicator, and "his famous phrase reflects a rhetorical technique that can be traced to ancient Greece—a figure of speech using three words to express one idea."[1]

The rule of three "suggests that things that come in threes are inherently funnier, more satisfying, or more effective than other numbers of things. The reader or audience of this form of text is also more likely to consume information if it is written in groups of threes."[2] Here are several examples:

Ready, set, go.
Lights, camera, action.
Reading, writing and arithmetic.
Blood, sweat and tears.
Father, Son and Holy Spirit.

Apply the Rule of Three—Part 1
I want to apply the rule of three to writing our mission statement.

1. *Talk it over.*
    If your kids are old enough, ask them to be involved. Generally speaking, people support what they help create, so involving your older children in the process may just help them buy into what you are building. Your end goal in writing your mission statement is to finish the following sentence: "Our family exists to . . ."
2. *Take your time.*
    It will take some time to come up with your family's mission statement, so don't feel like you need to get everything done in an hour—you can't. You don't want

to rush the process or force it. Ask for help; connect as a family; talk it over with your spouse. Let it marinate in your mind before you make your final choice. Once the statement moves from your head to your heart, you will know; then you are ready to trade in your pencil and eraser for a permanent pen.

3. *Think it through.*

You could say, "Our family lives to have fun." However, there are a few things wrong with this sort of mission statement. First, it's not measurable. Why are you just having fun? Where is the fun happening? How often do we have fun? Second, it's not specific. How will you have fun? Where will you have fun? Third, it's not very practical for everyday life. Your family exists to have fun? That's it? You can definitely include fun or happiness in your mission statement, but make the statement more specific.

As you do your thinking and discussing and writing, keep in mind these three things:

1. *Make it measurable.* Can you see what you want to do and where?
2. *Make it specific.* Say what needs to be said in three to four sentences.
3. *Make it practical.* Realistic directions to what you want to do.

Apply the Rule of Three—Part 2

Let's apply the rule of three another way. The following chart of verbs will serve as a source for finishing our statement. Of course, you don't need to use these exact words for your mission statement. I encourage you to do some exploring on your own as a family. But you are free to adopt any of the words here as well. As I mentioned above, we will start our statement with "Our family exists to . . ." Now we're going to add to the statement the three words from one of the columns in the chart and include them. Let's choose the three words in the first column.

Know	Listen	Encourage	Invest	Model
Grow	Learn	Equip	Instill	Move
Show	Live	Empower	Involve	Mentor

For the families who want to explore further, you can scour the Internet and Google "action verbs" and "rules of three" until you find what you are looking for. I will often sit down with a dictionary in one hand, yes, one made of paper, and a pen in the other, and make a list of words that rhyme, flow, or start with the same letter. A powerful website that can help you accomplish this is the One Look Dictionary System, *www.onelook.com*.

Our sample family mission statement now looks like this:

Our family exists to know, grow, show.

Not very dynamic, is it? Let's finish it up by adding a few words to make our mission more specific.

Ask and Answer Three Questions

Let me first remind you of our vision statement:

We are a family who does our absolute best for God and others.

Now, if you had to write a set of instructions to make your vision come together, what would you say? What words would you use? We are looking for three ways, three words or phrases, three actions that will explain our family's existence, that describe why we are here and what we will do to accomplish our vision. We're looking for three words that will make a huge difference in the life of our family, and depending on our mission, the lives of others. Here is an example of three questions you can ask for the words "know," "grow" and "show" in our mission statement:

1. What should we KNOW in order to do our absolute best for God and others?
2. What should we GROW in order to do our absolute best for God and others?
3. What should we SHOW in order to do our absolute best for God and others?

The chart below shows how each of the questions could be answered.

Know	God	Better
Grow	Family Relationships	Deeper
Show	Love	To Others

Now write your family mission statement by finishing the following phrase: "Our family exists to . . ." Include your three action words and your three specific words.

Our sample mission statement would then read: Our family exists to *know* God better, *grow* family relationships deeper, and *show* love to others.

Before moving on, set aside your statement and let it marinate in your mind. If it doesn't move your heart after a few days, make a few adjustments or go back to the beginning of this step and start again. It's better to take your time and get it right than be quick and get it wrong.

What We Have Accomplished

Foundation
"Whatever you do or say, do it as a representative of the Lord Jesus, giving thanks through him to God the Father" (Col. 3:17).

Vision
"We are a family who does our absolute best for God and others."

Mission
Our family exists to know God better, grow family relationships deeper, and show love to others.

Step 4: Defining My Family's Values

Verse to Remember
"Where there is no guidance the people fall, but in abundance of counselors there is victory" (Prov. 11:14, *NASB*).

Thoughts to Consider
Remember, our values are principles that guide our behavior and inform our decisions. What makes a value a true core value is whether or not it is actively influencing you to act and behave accordingly. If one of your core values is that "Honesty and integrity will guide our decisions," then when tax time rolls around, well, you know. Values only work when they tell us how to go about our daily lives and we listen and put them into action. When our values are in place and influencing our family behavior, a healthy culture will begin to develop. If values have not yet been part of your family, you will be in for a culture shock. Repetition creates habits and habits create culture. Your values are alive and working when your family can look at them and say, "This is the way we do things in our family." At that moment, you'll know that your values have been instilled into your family—but that takes time.

How many values to have is based on your unique family.

I would say between five and seven is a good number to have but there is no right or wrong answer. If you have too many values, you probably won't remember them. If you don't have enough, they won't be very helpful. You're the one who best can decide how many values will work for your family.

How you should write your values is up to you, but keep in mind that your goal is to have your values guide your decisions.

Here are three examples for you to consider as you think about how you can make your values easy to recall.

First Example: Attach Your Values to Your Family Name

If our goal is to have our values guide our decisions, then how important is it to remember them? Pretty important, right? For our family, we wrote our values into our last name. We did this to highlight our uniqueness, make our values memorable and give the added emotional component that says, "This is what guides the Jutila family." Notice the four characteristics of our list:

1. There are six values because there are six letters in our last name.
2. There is one word for each letter, so we can remember them.
3. There is a brief explanation of what each word means.
4. There is a verse that provides the basis for the value.

- **J***ust*. Do what is right and what is fair. "This is what the Lord requires from you: to do what is right, to love mercy, and to live humbly with your God" (Mic. 6:8, *GOD'S WORD*).
- **U***nderstand*. Put yourself in other people's shoes. "Don't look out only for your own interests, but take an interest in others, too" (Phil. 2:4).
- **T***hankful*. Be thankful in all situations. "Whatever happens, give thanks, because it is God's will in Christ Jesus that you do this" (1 Thess. 5:18, *GOD'S WORD*).
- **I***ntegrity*. Be honest and truthful in your behavior. "Finally, brothers and sisters, keep your thoughts on whatever is right or deserves praise: things that are true,

honorable, fair, pure, acceptable, or commendable"
(Phil. 4:8, *GOD'S WORD*).
- **L**augh. Have fun and enjoy life. "Being cheerful keeps
  you healthy. It is slow death to be gloomy all the time"
  (Prov. 17:22, *GNB*).
- **A**ble. Overcome life's obstacles and challenges. "I can
  do everything through Christ who strengthens me"
  (Phil. 4:13, *GOD'S WORD*).

Second Example: Attach Your Values to a Word

Think of a word that would be appropriate and memorable to attach your values to. Take the word "practice" for example. Practice is the custom or habit of doing something. That's a pretty good reminder for a core set of family values, don't you think? We want our values to be practiced daily until they become a habit. Notice the three characteristics of the list:

These values contain the following components:

1. There are eight values because there are eight letters
   in the word "practice."
2. There is one phrase for each letter.
3. The first word for each letter is a verb that ends in "ing."

1. **P**reparing children for their future.
2. **R**eplenishing life with uninterrupted time.
3. **A**ttending church together.
4. **C**reating environments where family feels comfortable.
5. **T**rusting God to accomplish the impossible.
6. **I**nvesting time to serve others.
7. **C**elebrating life with an attitude of thankfulness.
8. **E**ncouraging others with our words and actions.

Third Example: Write Out Your Values in Order of Importance

Another way to easily remember a list of values is to select five words that best describe your family and write them down in order of importance. This is the simplest way to write out your values, but don't equate simple with ineffective. Often times the simple way is the most effective way. If you want to write out your values this way, I would suggest you write a clarifying phrase or short explanation to make each value come alive.

1. Be honest.
2. Be authentic.
3. Be loyal.
4. Be available.
5. Be strong.

Actions to Take

Read through the following list of 75 values, highlighting the words that most resonate with your soul. Find words that you want to be part of your family's life as you plan for their future.

Accountability	Flexibility	Organization
Adventurousness	Friendliness	Passion
Ambition	Fun	Patience
Authenticity	Generosity	Peacefulness
Availability	Gratefulness	Persistence
Challenge	Growth	Practicality
Commitment	Happiness	Privateness
Competitiveness	Harmony	Proactivity
Connectedness	Helpfulness	Punctuality
Consistency	Honesty	Relationships
Cooperativeness	Honorability	Reliability

Courage	Hope	Resourcefulness
Creativity	Hospitality	Respect
Decisiveness	Humor	Sensitivity
Determination	Influence	Simplicity
Discipline	Innovation	Sincerity
Discovery	Integrity	Solitude
Empowerment	Intelligence	Stability
Enthusiasm	Justice	Strength
Encouragement	Knowledge	Thankfulness
Equipment	Leadership	Trust
Excellence	Learning	Truth
Fairness	Loyalty	Understanding
Faith	Openness	Variety
Fitness	Orderliness	Wisdom

From the words you highlighted, select the ones that you want most for your family and write them here in order of importance to your family. I have selected a few words to serve as an example.

- Excellence
- Organization
- Proactivity
- Resourcefulness
- Wisdom

Now, get creative with the words you have selected. Look back at the three examples we spoke about. In some way, can you use your family name or a powerful word to write your chosen values? For example: You may have noticed that the five words we selected from our list of 75 values begin with the letters *e, o, p, r* and *w*; and these letters can be rearranged to form the word "power." If not, maybe you can use synonyms for one or more of the chosen words in order to have the first letters make a word. After rearranging the letters, use a form of each word to create phrases that describe how your family wants to enact these values. The following examples show you what this looks like.

1. **P**roactive with opportunities
2. **O**rganized at home
3. **W**ise with finances
4. **E**xcellence in everything
5. **R**esourceful when challenged

What We Have Accomplished

Foundation
"Whatever you do or say, do it as a representative of the Lord Jesus, giving thanks through him to God the Father" (Col. 3:17).

Vision
"We are a family who does our absolute best for God and others."

Mission
Our family exists to know God better, grow family relationships deeper, and show love to others.

Values
Our family relies on God's power for life.

- **P**roactive with opportunities
- **O**rganized at home
- **W**ise with finances
- **E**xcellence in everything
- **R**esourceful when challenged

Step 5: Determining My Family's Goals

Verse to Remember

"Plans of the persistent surely lead to productivity, but all who are hasty will surely become poor" (Prov. 21:5, *ISV*).

Thoughts to Consider

Now that we have a firm foundation for our family, a vision of who we want our family to become, a mission that reminds us how we live life, and a core set of values that fuel our behavior, it's time to set a few goals to help us move forward. Our goals are the small steps we take to big impact. Before we get started, let's take a look at the example we have been using and see how far we have come in four steps.

Foundation

Whatever you do or say, do it as a representative of the Lord Jesus, giving thanks through him to God the Father (Col. 3:17).

Vision

We are a family who does our absolute best for God and others.

Mission

Our family exists to know God better, grow family relationships deeper, and show love to others.

Values

Our family relies on God's power for life.

- **P**roactive with opportunities
- **O**rganized at home
- **W**ise with finances
- **E**xcellence in everything
- **R**esourceful when challenged

Picture This

I'm sure you remember our five building blocks. You are working on the fifth one right now! If you recall, the picture we used looked like this.

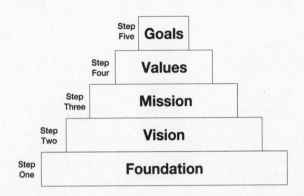

This picture shows the order of steps we need to take to build our family's future, starting with the foundation and ending with goals. However, once all the steps are completed, how the system works looks a little different. Let's merge what we have been working on together for the last four steps and take a look at how the system works. This will give us a better understanding of where our goals fit in the process. (See graphic on the next page.)

Looks a little different, doesn't it? The reason it looks different is because we had to develop our plan before we could reveal the process. We had to decide on a foundation before we designed our vision. We had to design a vision of what we wanted our family to become before we could describe our mission. We had to describe our family mission before we defined our core family values. And finally, we had to define our values before we could determine any goals. Now that we have everything in place, we can ask ourselves this very important question: *Why goals?* Good question. Goals help us progress toward our vision.

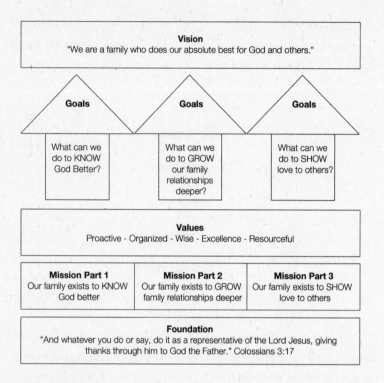

Notice the Change

If you look closely, you will notice only one major change in our plan and that is that we moved our vision to the top.

Here is the process:

- We stand on a firm foundation.
- We explain why we exist.
- We see our decisions through our core values.
- We set goals that flow from our mission.
- We accomplish goals to fulfill our vision.

So, how do we plan for our family's future?

We stand on a firm foundation and explain why our family lives their life. We make decisions through the lens of our core values because they influence our beliefs and fuel our behavior. We set goals that are aligned with our family mission and we do each of these things in order to become all that we want to become as a family, to accomplish our family's vision!

Actions to Take
Our goals should be in alignment with our mission, so that's where we will start. We will write one goal for each of the three areas of our mission statement so that we will know what to do in order to achieve the vision we have for our family.

Simplify the Mission Statement
The way to simplify your mission statement is to pick out the essential words.

The mission statement we're using as an example ("Our family exists to know God better, grow family relationships deeper, and show love to others") could be simplified to read:

- KNOW God better
- GROW family deeper
- SHOW love to others

Ask a Question
For each of the instructions in your mission statement, ask a question. For example:

- What can we do to know God better?
- What can we do to grow our family relationships deeper?
- What can we do to show love to others?

Rephrase the question to get a different perspective:

- Where can we know God better?
- When can we grow our family relationships deeper?
- Who can we show love to?

Write Your Goals

Get everyone in your family together. List each part of your mission statement across the top of separate pieces of paper. Select the area of your mission statement that you will focus on first. For example, we will write a goal that is in alignment with our mission to "grow our family relationships deeper." Ask the following question: "What can we do to grow our family relationships deeper?" Then let the ideas fly.

Mission:	Know God Better	Grow Family Deeper	Show Love to Others
Goals:		Have dinner together	
Goals:			
Goals:			
Goals:			

Okay, we have written a goal that will help us accomplish our vision. ("We are a family who does our absolute best for God and others.") We have stayed in alignment with our mission to "grow family relationships deeper." Now, let's review our goal. If you recall back in chapter 11, we talked about the five attributes of a well-written goal. We said goals must be . . .

- explainABLE
- attainABLE
- observABLE
- measurABLE
- adaptABLE

Now, let's take a look back at our goal and see how it matches up against the five attributes.

1. "Have dinner together." Is it explainable? Yes.
2. "Have dinner together." Is it attainable? Yes.
3. "Have dinner together." Is it observable? Yes.
4. "Have dinner together." Is it measurable? No.
5. "Have dinner together." Is it adaptable? Yes.

Did our goal pass the test? No. It didn't pass the test. It missed one key area. It wasn't measurable. You may think that having dinner together is measurable, because you can have a record that you had dinner together last Wednesday. Okay, that's fair. But what you are describing is "observable" not "measurable." Your goal is certainly observable: You said you wanted to have dinner together, and you did; you're done! Well, sort of. I applaud you for having dinner together, but you need to figure out how your goal can be adapted so that it's actually measurable. How about making the goal more specific? Here are three ways you can write this family goal and have it exhibit all five attributes of a well-written goal:

- Good: Have dinner together.
- Better: Have dinner together twice a week.
- Best: Have dinner together twice a week with everyone in our family present.

You can see as we move from good to better to best that we simply added language that allows us to measure the goal. As we added the language, we also made the goal more specific. If we say our goal is to have dinner together twice a week with everyone in our family present, then we have written a goal that answers what, how often and who will be there. Now you have a measurable goal!

What We Have Accomplished
Family, Inc. is just about ready to open its doors for business! Let's look back at our five steps to see what we have accomplished.

Foundation
Whatever you do or say, do it as a representative of the Lord Jesus, giving thanks through him to God the Father (Col. 3:17).

Vision
We are a family who does our absolute best for God and others.

Mission
Our family exists to know God better, grow family relationships deeper, and show love to others.

Values
Our family relies on God's power for life.

- **P**roactive with opportunities
- **O**rganized at home
- **W**ise with finances
- **E**xcellence in everything
- **R**esourceful when challenged

Goals
We have written a measurable goal for one area of our mission statement.

- KNOW God better.
- GROW family deeper: Have dinner together twice a week. with everyone in our family present.
- SHOW love to others.

Let me be the first to say, Congratulations! You have come a long way in planning and providing for the future of your family. This is a great moment to look back so that you can see what you have planned ahead: the vision for your family, your mission and your goals! They all point to a future filled with hope!

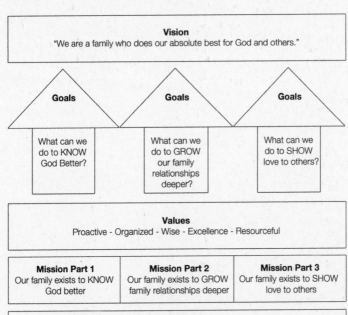

Vision
"We are a family who does our absolute best for God and others."

Goals

Goals

Goals

What can we do to KNOW God Better?

What can we do to GROW our family relationships deeper?

What can we do to SHOW love to others?

Values
Proactive - Organized - Wise - Excellence - Resourceful

Mission Part 1
Our family exists to KNOW God better

Mission Part 2
Our family exists to GROW family relationships deeper

Mission Part 3
Our family exists to SHOW love to others

Foundation
"And whatever you do or say, do it as a representative of the Lord Jesus, giving thanks through him to God the Father." Colossians 3:17

Final Thought

On more than one occasion while I wrote this book, I looked reflectively into my soul and asked myself, *Why are you writing a book on parenting? You have blown it more than once; you have let your anger get the best of you more than once. You have been emotionally disconnected more than once; and now, to top it all off, you have the audacity to give parenting advice to others?*

I hope you have understood that the information I've shared within these pages is not so much about always getting parenting right as much as it is about admitting when you've got it wrong, when you have made a mistake and when you need to correct your course and allow God's grace and mercy to show up.

I'm sure you have many of your own stories to tell, good and bad, funny and painful; but I hope you have seen yourself in some of the examples and illustrations from my life. As parents, we have hopes, dreams and aspirations for our kids. One day they will grow up and in all likelihood tell us they are doing something else with their lives, and the plans we had for them will not come to pass.

We must let them go and experience what God has called them to do. Believe it or not, He cares for them more than we do as parents. That is so hard for me to get my mind around sometimes because I care so much for my kids. I don't want them to experience hurt, pain, rejection and fear; yet everyone needs to "touch the stove" on occasion to see if it's hot. The least we can do as parents is see to it that we raise them the best we can so that when they touch the stove, they have a firm foundation that will give them stability and loving support.

My prayer is that this book has given you insight, perspective, understanding and, above all, hope! Hope in the Lord, hope in your children and hope in their future.

Above all else, live in a way that brings honor to the good news about Christ. Then, whether I visit you or not, I will hear that all of you think alike. I will know that you are working together and that you are struggling side by side to get others to believe the good news (Phil. 1:27, *CEV*).

Parenting together with you!
—Craig

Additional Resources

Four Steps on Your Faith Journey

Following are four lessons or four steps you can take with your child to get them talking about their faith journey. You can download these lessons and other resources to help your child on their faith journey at www.whowillyouempower.com/steps.

First Step to Know Christ
This step will introduce your child to Jesus and help you explain and understand what salvation means.

Next Step to Grow in Christ
This next step will help your child realize the importance of taking a few minutes a day to read God's Word, the Bible.

Step Up to Serve Christ
This third step takes your child a little further on his or her faith journey by talking about the importance of serving others.

Step Out to Share Christ
This fourth step will help your child to share his or her faith journey with others.

1. First Step to Know Christ
What Is Salvation?

Read the story about a man named Nicodemus in John 3:1-7, and then read the following paragraph:

Jesus told us that we must be "born again" in order to get to heaven. Well, we all know that we have been born once, since we are all here! What Jesus meant is that we must be born again into

His family. We must become children of God. How do we become born again? We get born again by asking Jesus to come and live in our hearts. We ask Jesus to come and live in our hearts by doing and remembering four things:

Number 1
The first thing we need to do is understand that God loves us! In fact, it says in John 3:16 that God loved us so much that He sent His only Son to die for us.

Number 2
The second thing we need to do is understand that we all sin. Sin means that we do not do what God wants us to do. Romans 3:23 in the Bible says that we all sin and that sin is the only thing that can keep us out of heaven.

Number 3
The third thing for us to understand is that even though we sin, God has provided a way for us to get to heaven—through His Son, Jesus. The Bible says in John 14:6 that the only way to get to heaven is through Jesus. We just need to ask Him to come and be that "way" for us. "How do you do that?" you ask. Check out the fourth and final step.

Number 4
The fourth thing we need to do is ask Jesus into our hearts by praying and inviting Him to come and live inside of us. Your prayer could go something like this: "Dear Jesus, I understand that I don't always do the things that You want me to do. I need Your help and I want You to be my Savior. Thank You for dying on the cross for all those sins I commit. Amen."

Each letter below has a phrase about salvation. Read the phrases and the verses, and write out the correct answer for each question.

Substitute for us
According to 1 Peter 2:24, what did Christ do with our sins?

_____

Abundant life
According to John 10:10, why did Jesus come to earth?

_____

Love of Christ
Read Romans 5:8. How did Christ show His love for us?

_____

Valuable gift
Romans 6:23 talks about a gift. What is the free gift of God?

_____

Accept Christ by faith
According to Ephesians 2:8-9, can good things get us into heaven?
Why or why not?

_____

Trust Christ
Read John 1:12. How do we become children of God?

_____

Invite Christ into your heart
Read Romans 10:9. How do we invite Christ into our hearts?

_____

Only one way to heaven
According to John 14:6, how many ways are there to get to heaven?
What is that one way?

_____

New life now in Christ
Read 2 Corinthians 5:17. Once we accept Christ, what do we become?

_____

Select one of the phrases from the word "SALVATION" above that is the most important to you and write it down. For example, you might choose the "S" phrase and write "substitute for us."

Why is this phrase important to you right now?

_____

_____

_____

In the word search below, circle the seven people or things that save lives.

DOCTOR
JESUS
LIFEGUARD
LIFE JACKET
LIFE PRESERVER
PARAMEDIC
SMOKE DETECTOR

```
A M X N A Z B C N S J D K L F P O J W E R J S
A L D K C M A N C J S K D P O E W K O S M F G
D K S M J O F K G K V S D O C T O R S K F Q B
D F N V O A J I M V I J P W O E R K X F M A D
S K N C S M O K E D E T E C T O R L A J S M S
P A R A M E D I C A M D J S K C P O S J D H E
A L K J F P Q W U E I T H S J A M X Z M C N C
A L D K S J C N M Z N A B S B C D J L D P O A
A M S L F K D P J E S U S A L D K A S P L X M
L I F E P R E S E R V E R A P W L S K D J M C
L I F A M S K L S K S A L I F E J A C K E T D
L A M C Z N C B H S L A P O Q W E R I A V N O
S D J F O A H F O I A G P I J P A N V K N P A
V D S F N F N L I F E G U A R D M V A J P G O
```

According to Romans 5:8, what did Jesus do to save lives?

_____

_____

_____

Select one verse below that you best understand, and memorize it this week.

John 14:6 (*NIV*):

"Jesus answered, 'I am the way and the truth and the life. No one comes to the Father except through me.'"

Romans 5:8 (*NIV*):

"But God demonstrates his own love for us in this: While we were still sinners, Christ died for us."

2 Corinthians 5:17 (*NIV*):

"Therefore, if anyone is in Christ, he is a new creation; the old has gone, the new has come!"

This verse is important to me because . . .

_____

_____

_____

_____

Action Step

My life will be different now that I know these things about salvation, because I will . . .

_____

_____

_____

_____

2. Next Step to Grow in Christ
What Is a Quiet Time?

You can download this lesson at
www.whowillyouempower.com/steps.

Let's take a quick minute and talk about attention. You know, the kind of attention adults like to talk about. In fact, maybe you have heard your mom or dad or even a teacher at school tell you to pay attention, or they may have asked you for your undivided attention. That means they really want you to listen or look and see what is going on. They want you to be focused. But let's face it: sometimes these things called interruptions get in our way of paying attention.

For example, suppose you have just gotten a brand-new video game. You are all set to try it out for the first time. You have been waiting all day, anticipating the very moment when you could dart out of school and get home to play the brand-new game. You start the game and watch as all the beginning graphics play. Just when all the cool graphics stop and you are ready to start playing, your best friend knocks at the door. Oh no! A huge interruption! The game no longer has your undivided attention. So you run and answer the door, you say you can't come outside right now, and you sit back down to start the game. All of a sudden the phone rings, and it's for you! Ahhh, another interruption. You talk on the phone with your friend for a few seconds and then go back to the game.

Well, I think you get the idea about interruptions and what paying attention means. We like to pay attention to our video games, and we certainly need to pay attention to our parents and teachers. But there is one other person we almost always forget to pay attention to, and that person is Jesus. One of the ways we can take time and pay attention to Jesus is through a quiet time. A quiet time is exactly that, a time to be quiet and read a couple of verses in the Bible and pray a simple prayer to God.

Take about 10 minutes right before you go to bed at night, and read your Bible and say a short prayer. Try not to have any interruptions, and for a few minutes pay attention only to God.

The phrases below describe what a quiet time is all about. Take a few minutes and answer the following questions.

Quiet time with God
Pick a time of the day or night that you can spend in a quiet time with God and write it here.
Time: _____

Understand God better
Reading the Bible and praying help us to understand God better. Choose a book in the New Testament, like Mark, that you will begin to read each day, and write that book name here.
Book: _____

Invest in your relationship with God
Since you have selected the book you are going to read in the New Testament, you will want to begin to read a chapter each day. This will help you invest in your relationship with God. Write down the date you started to read the book you chose.
Date: _____

Encouragement for right living
Reading God's Word encourages us to live the right way. Read Titus 2:11-12, and write down what that right way is.

_____

_____

Thank God for who He is
Read 1 Corinthians 15:57. What's one reason we have to thank God?

_____

_____

Talk to God through prayer

During your quiet time, you will want to spend a few minutes praying to God. Write down one prayer request you have.

_____

_____

_____

Important for growth

Read Psalm 1:2-3. What does this verse say we are like if we read God's Word?

_____

_____

_____

Memorize God's Word

Read Psalm 119:11. Why should we hide God's Word in our hearts (that means memorize Bible verses)?

_____

_____

_____

Establish a quiet time each day

It is very important to spend time with God every day. On the next page, for each day, write down the chapter you read, the verse that you thought was most important and one thing you learned.

_____

_____

_____

_____

Select one phrase from the words "QUIET TIME" above that is the most important to you and write it down. For example, you might choose the "E" phrase and write "establish a quiet time each day. This phrase is important to me because . . .

For each of the next five weekdays, try to spend 10 minutes reading God's Word and then pray a simple prayer to God. Finally, fill in the blank lines below for each day.

Monday
Chapter I read today: _____

Verse that was most important to me: _____

One important thing I learned: _____

_____

Tuesday
Chapter I read today: _____

Verse that was most important to me: _____

One important thing I learned: _____

_____

Wednesday
Chapter I read today: _____

Verse that was most important to me: _____

One important thing I learned: _____

_____

Thursday
Chapter I read today: _____

Verse that was most important to me: _____

One important thing I learned: _____

_____

Friday
Chapter I read today: _____

Verse that was most important to me: _____

One important thing I learned: _____

_____

Select one verse below that you best understand and memorize it this week.

1 Corinthians 15:57 (*NIV*):
"But thanks be to God! He gives us the victory through our Lord Jesus Christ."

Titus 2:12 (*NCV*):
"It teaches us not to live against God nor to do the evil things the world wants us to do. Instead, that grace teaches us to live in the present age in a wise and right way and in a way that shows we serve God."

Psalm 1:2 (*NCV*):
"They love the LORD's teachings, and they think about those teachings day and night."

I have memorized my verse and I have recited it to . . .

_____

This verse is important to me because . . .

_____

_____

_____

_____

Action Step

My life will be different now that I know these things about quiet time because I will . . .

_____

_____

_____

3. Step Up to Serve Christ
Serving Others

You can download this lesson at
www.whowillyouempower.com/steps.

Read Matthew 25:31-46.

The above verses are known as a parable. Many times Jesus would tell stories to make a point, and those stories are called parables. A parable is an earthly story with a heavenly meaning. This particular parable is called "The Parable of the Sheep and the Goats." In this story Jesus reminds us not only why we serve but who we serve.

Whenever we see people in need, we should do the best we can to serve them. We are reminded in this story that when we help those in need we are really serving God. Ephesians 6:7 tells us, "Do your work with enthusiasm. Work as if you were serving the Lord, not as if you were serving only men and women" (NCV).

Jesus even led us by example. He didn't come to this earth to be served but to serve others. We need to follow that example. Think for a minute about what ministry you are serving in.

Maybe you are serving the children's ministry by being a helper in a classroom. Maybe you are serving with your parents in a ministry by helping keep the church campus clean. Maybe you are serving as a greeter at a service. Or maybe, just maybe, you can't think of a ministry you are serving in.

I'm not talking about a one-time type of a ministry. You know, you stay after on Sunday to clean up the classroom because your leader asked you to. No, I'm talking about a regular ministry of service.

Service, you can say, is something you participate in on a weekly basis or every few days. For example, every Sunday morning you help with the puppet ministry at 11:00. You are on time, have the right attitude and want to serve.

If you think that you are not serving in a ministry, you are probably right and that's great! At least you realize it! The question now is, what are you going to do about it? We are going to spend the next few minutes exploring why we need to serve and how we can serve. As you work through this lesson, begin to think how you can best be used by God to serve others.

The phrases below talk about serving. Look up the verses and answer the questions.

Serve each other with the right attitude.
Read Galatians 5:13. According to this verse, what attitude should we have when we serve each other?

_____

_____

_____

_____

Example of service is Jesus.
According to Matthew 20:28, what was one of the reasons why Jesus came to the earth?

_____

_____

_____

Remember, we use our gifts to serve others.
First Peter 4:10 says that we all have received a gift from God. According to this same verse, how should we use our gift?

List three ways you can personally serve others this week.

1._____

2._____

3._____

Volunteer to serve with all your heart.
Romans 12:11 says, "Do not be lazy but work hard, serving the Lord with all your heart" (*NCV*). What does "serving the Lord with all your heart" mean?

_____

_____

_____

Enthusiastically serve the Lord.
Read Ephesians 6:7. When we serve others, whom are we really serving?

_____

_____

_____

Select one phrase from the word "SERVE" above that is most important to you and write it down. For example, you might choose the "S" for "serve each other with the right attitude."

Why is this phrase important to you right now?

_____

_____

_____

_____

_____

This phrase is important to me because . . .

_____

_____

_____

_____

_____

4. Step Out to Share
Share Your Faith

You can download this lesson at
www.whowillyouempower.com/steps.

Second Corinthians 5:19-20 says, "He gave us this message of peace. So we have been sent to speak for Christ. It is as if God is calling to you through us" (*NCV*).

What does "speak for Christ" mean? It means we need to be representatives for Christ. We are to represent Christ to those around us. If you were to look into a mirror, you would see an exact representation of yourself looking back at you. That's called a reflection. In the same way, we are to reflect or represent Christ to those around us—not only verbally, but also through our actions, attitude and character. That's what "speak for Christ" means.

Okay, now that we understand that, what is it that Christ would like to say through us? What is the message? I think the message is best summed up in 1 Corinthians 15:3-4: "I passed on to you what I received, of which this was most important: that Christ died for our sins, as the Scriptures say; that he was buried and was raised to life on the third day as the Scriptures say." That's it! It's as easy as one, two, three:

One: Jesus died for our sins.
Two: Jesus was buried.
Three: Jesus rose again on the third day.

Sometimes I think we try to make things too hard. It's really not. God's love is a free gift, and the only way to spend eternity with Him is to believe in the one-two-three we just discussed. For those of us who are already Christians, we have a responsibility to share that good news. Now we know what the good news is and we know that we are supposed to be sharing that good news with those around us. The next question is, what is the best way to share the good news?

I'm glad you asked. The two best ways to share Christ with others is through Scripture and through your own life. Check it out! The sentences below tell about sharing Christ with those around us. Look up the verses and answer the questions below.

Sharing Christ is something we must do.
Read 1 Corinthians 9:16. According to this verse, is sharing Christ with others an option?

_____

_____

He chose us to share the good news.
Read 1 Peter 2:9. What does it mean that God chose you?

_____

_____

Applying what we know is good.
Second Corinthians 5:18 says, "All this is from God. Through Christ, God made peace between us and himself, and God gave us the work of telling everyone about the peace we can have with him" (*NCV*). According to this verse, how can we apply God's peace?

_____

_____

Representing Christ is something we can do every day.
Read 2 Corinthians 5:19-20. What does "sent to speak for Christ" mean?

_____

_____

Explaining the good news is easy.
Read 1 Corinthians 15:1-4. List below the three parts of the good news. (Hint: They are found in verses 3 and 4.)

1._____

2._____
3._____

Answer the following questions on your own. Then share your answers with your parents. Sharing can be fun and easy. You just need to know what you are going to say!

The funniest thing that ever happened to me was . . .

_____
_____
_____
_____

My favorite color is . . .

_____
_____
_____
_____

My favorite hobby is . . .

_____
_____
_____

If I could be anything in the world, I would be . . .

_____
_____
_____
_____

My favorite subject in school is . . .

_____
_____
_____

Memorize 1 Corinthians 9:16 (*NCV*): "Telling the Good News is my duty—something I must do. And how terrible it will be for me if I do not tell the Good News."

I have memorized my verse and I have recited it to . . .

_____

Write the names of three people you will share Christ with during the next month. Share these names with your parents and your small group.

1._____

2._____

3._____

Rules for Maintaining a Healthy Social Media Account

1. You must "friend" Mom and Dad and keep us as "friends" at all times.
2. You must provide your social media password to Mom and Dad and let us know if you ever change it.
3. Do not "friend" anyone that you don't know personally. For example, don't "friend" another person's friend just because you know that other person.
4. Don't post a profile picture with someone other than a best friend, family member or pet. At some point your girlfriend or boyfriend is acceptable.
5. Don't "like" or comment on any post that will hurt someone else, hurt your parents or disappoint God.
6. Don't post any pictures of others without their permission—including a profile picture. Ask them first.
7. Don't "like" any websites, apps, music or videos that are inappropriate. If you don't know, then ask Mom or Dad.
8. Remember that future employers and universities often check social media sites when considering you for employment or enrollment when you are older.
9. Ask Mom and Dad if you have any questions or concerns about something on any social media site.
10. Think before you post anything. Things you post can exist forever online, even if you delete them right away. Someone could have taken a screen shot of your post and saved it. If you are not sure if you should post something, *don't* post it.

I understand these social media guidelines, and I also understand that if I break one of these rules my account(s) may be suspended as a consequence.

Child's Signature: _____ Today's Date: _____
Parent's Signature: _____ Today's Date: _____

Internet Safety Agreement

I promise to never give anyone my personal information or information about my family when I am online. Examples of my personal information include my name, age, address, telephone number, school or passwords.

I promise to never write anything mean or post any picture or video that hurts, humiliates or makes fun of others.

I promise to let my parents know if someone sends me a mean message and I promise not to respond to it.

I promise to only talk, text or chat with people I know and of whom my parents have approved.

I promise to always ask my parents before joining any site, club or social media site.

I promise to not click on any advertisements that may pop up on my screen or come to me in an email.

I promise to always tell my parents if I find anything that makes me uncomfortable while I am on the Internet, such as bad words, pictures or videos that make me afraid or uncomfortable.

I know that my parents will be checking my Internet steps and other digital places I visit to keep me safe.

Child's Signature: _____ Today's Date: _____
Parent's Signature: _____ Today's Date: _____

Cell Phone Responsibility Agreement*

Normal Use

❑ I will not text or place phone calls between ___:____P.M. and
   ___:____A.M.

❑ I will send no more than _____ texts per day.

❑ I will not exceed my allotted monthly minutes or text message
limits.

❑ I will charge my phone in an open space and not in my room.

Safety

❑ I will answer my phone when my parent calls.

❑ I will not download or subscribe to anything on my phone without parental permission.

❑ I will not disable any parental controls on my phone.

❑ I will tell my parents when I receive inappropriate texts or sexts.

❑ I will tell my parents if I am being harassed by someone on my cell phone.

❑ I will not harass or bully anyone with my cell phone.

❑ I will not use my cell phone to arrange meetings with anyone my parents don't know.

Texting

❑ I will not send threatening or mean texts to others.

❑ I will not take or send embarrassing photos of myself, my family or my friends.

❑ I will not share photos with other people without their permission.

❑ I will not text messages about people in a way that hurts their reputation.

❑ I will not forward a hurtful message or picture sent to me about someone else.

Being Polite

❑ I will not bring my cellphone anywhere that my parents prohibit its use, like the family dinner table.

❑ I will not be rude to others by talking or texting in public places where cell phone use is not allowed or is inappropriate, like in a church or a library.

❑ I will follow all school rules about cell phone use.

The following are reasonable consequences if any of the above rules are broken.

Consequences

❑ I understand that having a cell phone is a privilege that can be taken away.

❑ I understand this agreement will help me to demonstrate responsible behavior.

❑ I understand my parents reward good behavior with more freedom.

❑ I understand there are consequences for breaking this agreement.

Parent Responsibilities

❑ I will answer any questions my child has about owning a cell phone.

❑ I will periodically revisit these rules as my child gets older and technology evolves.

❑ I will not take away my child's cell phone if he [or she] comes to me regarding inappropriate content received from someone else.

Child's Signature: _____ Today's Date: _____

Parent's Signature: _____ Today's Date: _____

---

* Agreement adapted from "Cellphone Usage Contract," *ROCK*, April 8, 2011. http://www.myrocktoday.com/default.asp?q_areaprimaryid=7&q_areasecondaryid=75&q_areatertiaryid=63&q_articleid=894 (accessed June 2013).

Endnotes

Introduction: Parenting Your Modern Family

1. Bill Wrubel, "The Bicycle Thief," *Modern Family*, season 1, episode 2, directed by Jason Winer, aired September 30, 2010 (Los Angeles, CA: 20th Century Fox, 2010), DVD.

Chapter 1: Set a Healthy Life Pace

1. Don Tapscott, "How to Teach and Manage 'Generation Net'" *Business Week Online*, November 30, 2008. www.businessweek.com/technology/content/nov2008/tc30081130_713563.htm. Quoted in Nicholas Carr, *The Shallows: What the Internet Is Doing to Our Brains* (New York: W. W. Norton & Company, 2010), Kindle ed.
2. Christopher Lloyd, Steven Levitan and Bill Wrubel, "Someone to Watch over Lily," *Modern Family*, season 2, episode 20, directed by Michael Spiller, aired April 20, 2011 (Los Angeles, CA: 20th Century Fox, 2011), DVD.
3. Legacy Countdown, The ReThink Group, https://itunes.apple.com/us/app/legacy-countdown/id635713919?mt=8 (accessed June 2013). You'll find this app available online at the Apple store.
4. Story adapted from "The Whole World Came Together," *The 30 Best Inspiring Anecdotes of All Times*, 1998-99. http://www.businesslead.com/msb/anecdotes.htm (accessed August 2012).
5. Voltaire, *Yahoo! Answers*. http://answers.yahoo.com/question/index?qid=20070107135 519AAUe5TB (accessed May 2013).
6. James Dobson, *Solid Answers* (Wheaton, IL: Tyndale, 1997), pp. 105-106.
7. Carol Sorgen, "Cut the Stress, Simplify Your Life," WebMD, 2006. http://www.webmd.com/a-to-z-guides/features/cut-stress-simplify-life (accessed May 2013).
8. Christopher Lloyd and Steven Levitan, "Pilot," *Modern Family*, season 1, episode 1, directed by Jason Winer, aired September 23, 2009 (Los Angeles, CA: 20th Century Fox, 2010), DVD.

Chapter 2: Plan Moments of Rest

1. *Dictionary.com*, s.v. "balance." http://dictionary.reference.com/browse/balance?&o=100074 &s=t (accessed May 12, 2013).
2. Ibid.
3. Jackson Browne, "Running on Empty" (released 1977, Asylum, B004ER1MZW,331/3 rpm. http://www.azlyrics.com/lyrics/jacksonbrowne/runningonempty.html (accessed January 2014).
4. L. B. Cowan, *Streams in the Desert* (Grand Rapids, MI: Zondervan, 1997), Kindle ed.
5. Dr. Archibald Hart, *Adrenaline and Stress* (Nashville, TN: Thomas Nelson Inc., 1995), Kindle ed.
6. Dr. Archibald Hart, *Thrilled to Death: How the Endless Pursuit of Pleasure Is Leaving Us Numb* (Nashville, TN: Thomas Nelson, 2007), Kindle ed.

Chapter 3: Schedule Uninterrupted Time Together

1. Google Calendar is available for free at https://www.google.com/calendar.
2. An overview of the calendar app that comes loaded on an Apple computer (iCal) is available at http://www.apple.com/osx/apps/#calendar.
3. Cozi is available for free at http://www.cozi.com/.
4. Cyril Northcote Parkinson, "Parkinson's Law," *The Economist*, November 19, 1955. http://www.economist.com/node/14116121 (accessed January 2014).

5. Nicholas Carr, *The Shallows: What the Internet Is Doing to Our Brains* (New York: W. W. Norton & Company, 2010), Kindle ed.

6. *Dictionary.com*, s.v. "distracted." http://dictionary.reference.com/browse/distracted?s=t (accessed December 2012).

7. A. T. Robertson, *Word Pictures in the New Testament—Luke, Christian Classics Ethereal Library*. http://www.ccel.org/ccel/robertson_at/wp_luke.xi.html (accessed December 2012).

8. John Gill, *Exposition of the Entire Bible, Internet Sacred Texts Archive,* quoted at *Bible Hub,* 2004-2013. http://gill.biblecommenter.com/luke/10.htm (accessed June 2013).

Chapter 4: Model the Behavior You Want

1. Gilda Radner, *It's Always Something* (New York: Simon and Schuster, 1989), pp. 268-269.

2. Catherine Aird, *Catherine Aird*. http://www.catherineaird.com (accessed July 2013).

3. Kendra Cherry, "What Is Short Term Memory," *About.com, Psychology*. http://psychology.about.com/od/memory/f/short-term-memory.htm (accessed July 2013).

4. Elaine Minamide, *Impressionable Minds, Focus on the Family,* August 2002, pp. 2-3, quoted at *Focus on the Family Africa*. http://www.safamily.co.za/?showarticles&global%5B_id%5D=615 (accessed July 2013).

5. Meredith F. Small, "More than the Best Medicine," *Scientific American*, August 2000, p. 24.

6. *The Free Dictionary,* s.v. "rhythm." http://www.thefreedictionary.com/rhythm (accessed July 2013).

Chapter 5: Repeat the Behavior You Want

1. Charles Isbell, "Deuteronomy's Definition of Jewish Learning," *Jewish Bible Quarterly*, vol. 31, no. 2 (2003). http://www.jbq.jewishbible.org/assets/Uploads/312/312_DEUTERO3.pdf (accessed June 2013).

2. *Urbandictionary.com*, s.v. "peerent." http://www.urbandictionary.com/define.php?term=peerent (accessed June 2013)

3. Christopher Lloyd and Steven Levitan, "The Incident," *Modern Family*, season 1, episode 4, directed by Jason Winer, aired October 14, 2009 (Los Angeles, CA: 20th Century Fox, 2010), DVD.

4. B. Fiese, K. Foley and M. Spagnola, "Routine and Ritual Elements in Family Mealtimes: Contexts for Child Well-Being and Family Identity," *New Directions for Child and Adolescent Development* (2006) 111, 67-89, cited at Eliza Cook and Rachel Dunifon, "Do Family Meals Really Make a Difference?" *Parenting In Context, Cornell University College of Human Ecology* (Cornell Cooperative Extension, 2012). http://www.human.cornell.edu/pam/outreach/parenting/research/upload/Family-Mealtimes-2.pdf (accessed June 2013).

5. Ann Meier and Kelly Musick, "Is the Family Dinner Overrated?" *The New York Times Sunday Review,* June 29, 2012. http://www.nytimes.com/2012/07/01/opinion/sunday/is-the-family-dinner-overrated.html?_r=0 (accessed May 2013).

6. Jeanie Lerche Davis, "Family Dinners Are Important," Information and Resources, *WebMD,* 2006. http://www.webmd.com/a-to-z-guides/features/family-dinners-are-important (accessed June 2013).

7. Michele Weiner-Davis, "Time Together," *Divorce Busting,* 2009. http://www.divorcebusting.com/a_time_together.htm (accessed June 2013).

8. Rick Riordan. Goodreads.com. http://www.goodreads.com/quotes/tag/children (accessed June 2013).

Chapter 6: Reinforce the Behavior You Want

1. *Biblicaltraining.org*, s.v. "phylactery." http://www.biblicaltraining.org/library/phylactery (accessed May 2013).

2. Ashley Crossman, "Charles Horton Cooley," *About.com*, 2013. http://sociology.about.com/od/Profiles/p/Charles-Horton-Cooley.htm (accessed January 2014).

3. William L. Cook and Emily M. Douglas, "The Looking-Glass Self in Family Context: A Social Relations Analysis," *Journal of Family Psychology*, v. 12, no. 3, September 1998, pp. 299-309.

4. Les and Leslie Parrot, "Fighting Through the Big Five," *The Huffington Post*, May 21, 2013. http://www.huffingtonpost.com/les-and-leslie-parrott/fighting-through-the-big-five_b_3308657.html (accessed July 2013).

5. Christopher Lloyd and Steven Levitan, "Earthquake," *Modern Family*, season 2, episode 3, directed by Michael Spiller, aired October 6, 2010 (Los Angeles, CA: 20th Century Fox, 2011), DVD.

6. "Dr. Paul Brand CBE," *The Leprosy Mission: England and Wales, 2013*. http://www.leprosymission.org.uk/about-us-and-leprosy/our-history/paul-brand.aspx (accessed July 2013).

7. Anjali Kulkarni, Jaya Shankar Kaushik, Piyush Gupta, Harsh Sharma and R. K. Agrawal, "Massage and Touch Therapy in Neonates: The Current Evidence," *Indian Pediatrics*, vol. 47, no. 17, 2010. http://medind.nic.in/ibv/t10/i9/ibvt10i9p771.pdf (accessed July 2013).

8. Daniel Goleman, *Emotional Intelligence* (New York: Bantam, 1995), p. 80.

9. Kathleen Parker, "Let's Give Our Boys a Gift: Self Control," *USA Today*, September 15, 1999, sec. A, p. 17A.

10. Lao Tzu, BrainyQuote.com. http://www.brainyquote.com/quotes/quotes/l/laotzu137141.html (accessed June 2013).

11. "Bamboo in Daily Life," *Espace pour la Vie Montréal, The Chinese Garden of the Montreal Botanical Garden*. http://www2.ville.montreal.qc.ca/jardin/en/chine/bambou/floraison.htm (accessed June 2013).

Chapter 7: Protect Your Child Online

1. "Online Safety for Kids," *FindLaw*, 2013. http://family.findlaw.com/parental-rights-and-liability/online-safety-for-kids.html (accessed August 2012).

Chapter 8: Set Digital Boundaries

1. Cara Brull, email message to author, January 19, 2013. Used by permission.

2. "Proverbs 22:3," *Biblos.com*, 2004-2013. http://biblelexicon.org/proverbs/22-3.htm (accessed May 2013).

3. *Biblos.com*, s.v. "panourgos." http://biblesuite.com/greek/3835.htm (accessed May 2013).

4. "Fools," World of Quotes, 2013. http://www.worldofquotes.com/topic/fools/1/index.html (accessed June 2013).

5. K. Tsubota and K. Nakamori, "Dry Eyes and Video Display Terminals," *New England Journal of Medicine*, 328, 1993, pp. 584-585, quoted at "Computer Vision Syndrome (CVS): Dry Eye," *EyeScience.org*. http://www.eyescience.org/ (accessed June 2013).

6. Nicholas Carr, *The Shallows: What the Internet Is Doing to Our Brains* (New York: W. W. Norton & Company, 2010), Kindle ed.

7. Ibid.

8. Ibid.

9. Lynn Langton, "Identity Theft Reported by Households, 2005-2010," *Bureau of Justice Statistics*, November 30, 2011. http://www.bjs.gov/index.cfm?ty=pbdetail&iid=2207 (accessed May 2013).

10. Christopher Lloyd and Steven Levitan, "The Kiss," *Modern Family*, season 2, episode 2, directed by Scott Ellis, aired September 29, 2010 (Los Angeles, CA: 20th Century Fox, 2011), DVD.

11. Ibid.

12. "Internet Monitoring: Dad and Son," *Your Teen* magazine, January 5, 2012. http://yourteenmag.com/2012/01/internet-monitoring-dad-and-son/ (accessed July 2013).
13. "Monitoring Teenagers Internet Use," *Your Teen* magazine, March 16, 2012. http://yourteenmag.com/2012/03/monitoring-teenagers-internet-use (accessed May 2013).
14. Keith Kanner, "Internet Monitoring: Privacy vs. Safety," *Young Teen* magazine, January 5, 2012. http://yourteenmag.com/2012/01/internet-monitoring-privacy-vs-safety/ (accessed May 2013).

Chapter 9: Keep Communication Open

1. Christopher Lloyd and Steven Levitan, "Pilot," *Modern Family*, season 1, episode 1, directed by Jason Winer, aired September 23, 2009 (Los Angeles, CA: 20th Century Fox, 2010), DVD.
2. Daniel Weiss, "The New Normal? Youth Exposure to Online Pornography," April 6, 2011. http://myrocktoday.com/default.asp?q_areaprimaryid=7&q_areasecondary id=74&q_areatertiaryid=0&q_articleid=861 (accessed August 29, 2012), quoting Janis Wolak, Kimberly Mitchell and David Finkelhor, "Unwanted and Wanted Exposure to Online Pornography in a National Sample of Youth Internet Users," *Pediatrics*, vol. 119, no. 2 (February 2007), p. 251.
3. David Sarnoff (speech at Notre Dame University, 1955), quoted in Nicholas Carr, *The Shallows: What the Internet Is Doing to Our Brains* (New York: W. W. Norton & Company, 2010), Kindle ed.
4. Minara El-Rahman, "Cyberbullying: A Rundown of Cyberbullying Laws," FindLaw, January 27, 2010. blogs.findlaw.com/law_and_life/2010/01/cyberbullying-suicide-shows-need-for-cyberbullying-laws.html (accessed June 2013).
5. "Prevent Your Child from Being a Victim of Cyberbullying." *Marina Times*, vol. 28, no. 9, September 2011. http://www.marinatimes.com/sep11/athome_familymatters2.html (accessed August 2012).
6. Mahdieh Darehzereshki, "Cyber Bullying State Laws and Policies," Cyberbullying, May 26, 2010. http://cyber-bulling.blogspot.com/2010/05/cyberbullying-state-laws-and-policies.html (accessed June 2013).
7. *Sex and Tech: Results from a Survey of Teens and Young Adults*, The National Campaign to Prevent Teen and Unplanned Pregnancy, 2008. http://www.thenationalcampaign.org/sextech/PDF/SexTech_Summary.pdf (accessed July 2013).
8. Ibid.
9. Mike Celizic, "Her Teen Committed Suicide Over 'Sexting'" *Today*, March 6, 2009. http://www.today.com/id/29546030/ns/today-parenting_and_family/t/her-teen-committed-suicide-over-sexting (accessed July 2013).
10. Deborah Feyerick and Sheila Steffen, "'Sexting' Lands Teens on Sex Offender List." CNN, 2013. http://www.cnn.com/2009/CRIME/04/07/sexting.busts (accessed July 2013).
11. "Perils of Sexting: Teens Face Child Porn Charges," Today.com, from Internet Archive, March 2009, MPEG Video, 7:14. http://www.today.com/video/today/29613004#29613004 (accessed July 2013).
12. Adapted from "Tips to Prevent Sexting," National Center for Missing and Exploited Children: NetSmatz Workshop, 2009. http://www.doj.state.wi.us/sites/default/files/dci/icac/sexting-prevention.pdf (accessed January 2014).
13. "Generation M2: Media in the Lives of 8- to 18-Year-Olds," The Henry J. Kaiser Foundation, January 20, 2010, p. 18. http://kaiserfamilyfoundation.files.wordpress.com/2013/04/8010.pdf (accessed July 2013).

Chapter 10: Establish Your Family's Purpose

1. Roger Lancelyn Green, ed., *The Works of Lewis Carroll* (London: Spring Books, 1965), p. 65.
2. "Mission Statement," *The Economist*, 2013. http://www.economist.com/node/13766375 (accessed June 2013).

3. Christopher Lloyd and Steven Levitan, "Family Portrait," *Modern Family*, season 1, episode 24, directed by Jason Winer, aired May 19, 2010 (Los Angeles, CA: 20th Century Fox, 2010), DVD.

Chapter 11: Determine Your Family's Priorities

1. "Roy Disney Quotes," *ThinkExist.com*, 1999–2013. http://en.thinkexist.com/quotes/Roy_Disney (accessed May 2013).
2. David Grusenmeyer, "Mission, Vision, Values and Goals," *Michigan State University Extension*, p. 3. https://www.msu.edu/~steind/estate%20Goals%20Mission%20Values%20Overview_ProDairy%2017pg.pdf (accessed July 2013).
3. "Tom Landry Quotes," *BrainyQuote* 2001–2013. http://www.brainyquote.com/quotes/authors/t/tom_landry.html (accessed July 2013).
4. Sam Walton, *Sam Walton: Made in America* (New York: Bantam Books, 1993), p. 28.

Chapter 12: Design Your Family's Process

1. Carmine Gallo, "Thomas Jefferson, Steve Jobs, and the Rule of 3," *Forbes*, July 2, 2012. http://www.forbes.com/sites/carminegallo/2012/07/02/thomas-jefferson-steve-jobs-and-the-rule-of-3/ (accessed August 2013).
2. Wikipedia, s.v. "rule of three," November 29, 2013. http://en.wikipedia.org/wiki/Rule_of_three_%28writing%29 (accessed August 2013).

Acknowledgments

This book would not have been possible without the great parents and great friends I have come to know over the years. Throughout the writing of *Faith and the Modern Family*, each of the parents listed below gave insight, suggestions, feedback and occasionally loving pushback to make sure the content was not only as accurate as it could be, but also as authentic as it could be. They have watched Mary and me parent, they have cheered our successes, and they have witnessed our failures—yet they love us anyway.

Proverbs 24:6 says that "victory depends on having many advisers." My friends, my examples and my advisers are the reason this book exists. Huge blessings to them!

Chris and Dawn Lewis—We have been through so much over the years, and through it all our friendship has not only remained strong but also has deepened. You were there when our twins were born and we were there for yours! Thanks for your editing, counsel and for pushing me on the hard issues. You guys are amazing.

Martin and Debbie Lombrano—My life is richer and deeper because of watching, listening to and laughing with you two. Sharing struggles and accountability has made me better as a husband and a dad, and the almost daily texts from Martin lift my spirit and make me a better person.

Doah and Chrisy Lynd—"Deep," "transparent," "compassionate" and "fun" are four words that come to mind when I think of you. You have been consistent prayer warriors for us and our family and have mentored our kids. Thank you for your insight and the way you do life as a family. We are eternally grateful for you!

Ed and Dolly McGuigan—Not only are you lifelong friends, but also as a speaking mentor and "theological thought leader," you have never stopped building into my life. We have laughed a lot and cried a little. Thank you for making a huge difference in my life and for "helping me clear my plate."

Joe and Janet Moser—You two are such encouraging and uplifting people. You have built into my life and you have built up my life. Your influence on this book is profound. Thank you for the richness of your friendship and your Godly advice.

John and Debbie Reed—You guys are amazing friends with powerful insight and wisdom. Thank you for giving me the opportunity to introduce this at TerraNova Church before it became a book! You helped me fine-tune the words and I am deeply grateful.

J and Cheri Steele—It helps to share the depths and occasional disappointments of our parenting journey with others, and we have had shared some depth! You have helped me to be a better parent by allowing us to watch how you talk to and encourage your kids. Thank you for encouraging us on this sometimes-tough parenting road.

Mike and Lorie Taylor—You are both amazing parents with great insight and I appreciate the practical application you brought to this book! Your ideas were terrific and your feedback helped shape the critical content of this book. Thank you for your powerful investment.

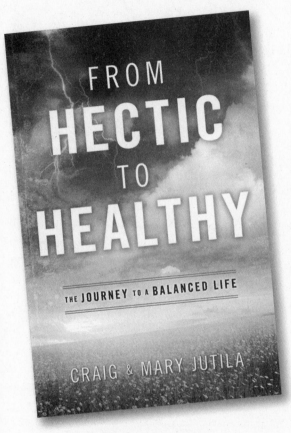